WITH
POOR EMIGRANTS
TO AMERICA

WITH
POOR EMIGRANTS
TO AMERICA

BY

STEPHEN GRAHAM

AUTHOR OF "WITH THE RUSSIAN PILGRIMS
TO JERUSALEM"

THOMAS NELSON AND SONS, Ltd.
LONDON, EDINBURGH, AND NEW YORK

NOTE.

A TRANSLATION of this book has appeared serially in Russia before publication in Great Britain and America. The matter has accordingly been copyrighted in Russia.

My acknowledgments are due to the Editor of *Harper's Magazine* for permission to republish the story of the journey.

I wish to express my thanks to Mrs. James Muirhead, Miss M. A. Best, and to Mr. J. Cotton Dana, who, with unsparing energy and hospitality, helped me to see America as she is.

STEPHEN GRAHAM.

VLADIKAVKAZ, RUSSIA.

CONTENTS.

PROLOGUE.

————◆◆————

FROM Russia to America; from the most backward to the most forward country in the world; from the place where machinery is merely imported or applied, to the place where it is invented; from the land of Tolstoy to the land of Edison; from the most mystical to the most material; from the religion of suffering to the religion of philanthropy.

Russia and America are the Eastern and Western poles of thought. Russia is evolving as the greatest artistic philosophical and mystical nation of the world, and Moscow may be said already to be the literary capital of Europe. America is showing itself as the site of the New Jerusalem, the place where a nation is really in earnest in its attempt to realise the great dream of human progress. Russia is the living East; America is the living West—as India is the dead East and Britain is the dying West. Siberia will no doubt be the West of the future.

For one who knows Russia well America is full of a great revelation. The contrast in national spirit is so sharp that each helps you to see the other more clearly. The American people are now on the threshold of a great progressive era; they feel themselves within sight of the realisation of many of their ideals. They have been hampered badly by the trusts and the " bosses " and the corrupt police, but they are now proving that these obstacles are

I a

merely temporary anomalies, caused by the overwhelmingly sudden growth of population and prosperity. A few years ago it could with truth be said that material conditions were worse in the United States than in the Old World. But it has been clear all the time that the corruption existent in the country was truly foreign to the country's temper.

The common citizen is becoming the watch-dog of the police-service. Tammany has fallen. Women are getting the suffrage, state by state. The nation is unanimous in its cry for a pure state, a clean country, and an uncorrupted people. All diseases are to be healed. Couples who wish to be married must produce health-certificates. The mentally deficient and hereditary criminals are to be segregated. Blue-books, or rather what the Americans call White-books, are going to form the Bible of a new nation. The day is going to be *rationally* divided into eight hours' work, eight hours' pleasure, eight hours' sleep—or rather, eight hours' looking at machinery, eight hours' pleasure, eight hours' sleep, for machinery is going to accomplish all the ugly toil. Everybody is to be well dressed, well housed, comfortable. America is raging against drink, against the exploitation of immigrants, against the fate of the white slave, against any one who has done anything immoral. It will nationally expel a Russian genius like Gorky. It makes great difficulty of admitting to its shores any one who has ever been in prison. It is so in earnest about the future of America that it has set up what is almost an insult to Europe—the examination of Ellis Island. Any one who has gone through the ordeal of the poor emigrant, as I did, going into America with a party of poor Russians in the steerage, and has been medically examined and clerically cross-questioned about his life and ethics, knows that America is a materialist and progressive country, and that she is no longer a harbour of refuge for the weak, but a place where a nation is determined to have health and strength and prosperity.

Now in Russia, when you arrive there, you find no such tyranny as that of Ellis Island awaiting you. You have come to the land of charity. If there is any question it is of whether you are a Russian Jew wanting to be recognised as an American citizen. Their charity does not extend to the Jews. But disease does not stand in your way, neither does crime ; ethics are not inquired into ; Mylius or Mrs. Pankhurst or Miss Marie Lloyd receive their passports without a frown. You have come to the nation to whom are precious the sick, the mentally deficient, the criminal, the waste-ends of humanity, the poor woman on the streets, the drunkard. Her greatest novelist, Dostoievsky, was an epileptic ; her national poet, Nekrasof, was a drunkard ; Vrubel, one of her greatest painters, was an imbecile ; Chekhof, her great tale-writer, was a hopeless consumptive. She is not opposed to the good and the sound, but the suffering are dearer to her, more comprehensible. She loves the drunkard, and says " Yes, you are right to be drunk ; you are probably a good man. It is what you are likely to be in this world of enigmas." She loves the white slave, but does not wish to shut her in a home for such. The Russians, so far from segregating the diseased and the fallen, frequently fall in love with them and marry them. They are sorry for the crippled children, but do not wish they had never been born. They see in them a reminder of the true lot of man upon the world. They make such children holy, and set them at the church doors. Russia does not execute the murderer except under martial law, but she sends him to Siberia to understand life and be *resurrected*. Thus, in *The Crime and Punishment*, Raskolnikof, the murderer, goes to Siberia with little Sonia, the white slave, who whispers to him all the way the promises of St. John's Gospel.

In America the man who is tramping the road and will not work is an object of enmity. He is almost a criminal. He is not wanted. He will receive little hospitality, must chop wood for his breakfast or steal. His life is a blasphemy breathed against the American ideal. But in Russia none is looked upon more kindly than the man on the road, the tramp or the pilgrim. There are a million or so of them on the road in the summer. They are characteristic of Russia. In them the Russian confesses that he is a stranger and a pilgrim upon the earth.

The Christianity of Russia is the Christianity of death, of renunciation, of what is called the *podvig*, the turning away from the empire of "the world" as proposed by Satan on the mountain, the wasting of the ointment rather than the raising of the poor, the giving the lie to Satan, the part of Mary rather than the part of Martha.

But the Christianity of America is the Christianity of Life, of affirmation, of "making good," of accepting "the world" and preparing for Christ's second coming, of obedience to the law, of almsgiving. America is the great almsgiver, appealed to for money from the ends of the earth, and for every object. If Russia can give faith, America can give the rest. It is impossible for America to say with St. Peter "Silver and gold have I none, but *such as I have* give I thee." The Americans believe in money, and the pastor of a fashionable church is able to say, "I preach to fifty million dollars every Sunday morning." But as Mme. Novikof, in one of her brilliant conversations, once said, "What is greater than the power of money? Why, contempt of money." There are no people in the world who keep fewer account-books than the Russians. They fling about their wealth or the pennies of their poverty with the generous assurance that the bond of brotherhood is greater than their fear of personal deprivation.

The Americans are great collectors. It may be said collecting is the genius of the West ; empty-handedness is the glory of the East.

The Russians are a sad and melancholy people. But they do not want to lose their melancholy or to exchange it for Western self-satisfaction. It is a divine melancholy. As their great contemporary poet Balmont writes :

I know what it is to moan endlessly—
In the long cold Winter to wait in vain for Spring,
But I know also that the nightingale's song is beautiful to us
    just because of its sadness,
And that the silence of the snowy mountain peaks is more
    beautiful than the lisping of streams—

which is somewhat of a contrast to a conversation reported in one of Professor Jacks' books :

Passenger, looking out of the train window at the snowy ranges of the Rockies : " What mountains ! "

American, puzzled for a moment : " I guess I h'ant got any use for those, but ef you're thinking of buying real estate. . . ."

The phrase, *real estate !*

Britain is seated in the mean. Compared with America she is semi-Eastern. Despite the blood-relationship of the American and British peoples they are more than an ocean apart. We receive without much thanks American songs and dances, boxers, Carnegie libraries, and plenty of money for all sorts of purposes. But our backs are to America ; we look towards Russia and are all agog about the next Russian book or ballet or music. We are an old nation ;

as far as the little island is concerned hope has died down.
We have explored the island. America will take a long
time to explore *her* territory. No vast tracts and inex-
haustible resources and terrific upheavals of Nature reflect
themselves in our national mood. The American working
man has a true passion for work, for his country, for everything; the British working man does his duty. We have
not the belief in life that the American has—we have not
yet the Russian's belief in death.

The American breathes full into his lungs the air of life.
The American is glad at the sight of the strong, the victorious, the healthful. How often, in novels and in life,
does the American woman, returning from a sojourn in the
far West, confess to her admiration of the cowboy! She
is thrilled by the sight of such strong wild " husky " fellows,
each of them equal to four New Yorkers. In England,
however, the town girl has no smiles for the strong peasant;
he is a country bumpkin, no more. She wants the ideal,
the unearthly. In Russia weakness attracts far more than
strength; love is towards consumptives, cripples, the half-
deranged, the impossibles. The Americans do not want
the weak one; England backs the " little un " to win;
Russia loves the weak one, feeling he will be eternally
beaten, and loves him because he will be beaten. But
America loves the strong, the healthy, the pure, because
she is tired of Europe and the weakness and disease and
sorrow of Europeans.

WITH POOR EMIGRANTS TO AMERICA.

I.

THE VOYAGE.

AT Easter 1912 I was with seven thousand Russian peasants at the Holy Sepulchre in Jerusalem. On Easter Day 1913 I arrived with Russian emigrants at New York, and so accomplished in two consecutive years two very different kinds of pilgrimage, following up two very significant life-movements in the history of the world of to-day. One of these belongs to the old life of Europe, showing the Middle Ages as it still survives under the conservative regime of the Tsars ; the other is fraught with all the possibilities of the future in the making of the New America.

It was in March that I decided to follow up the movements of the people out of the depths of Europe into America, and with that purpose sought out I—— K——, a well-known immigration agent in the East End of London. He transshipped Russians coming *via* Libau and London, and could tell me just when he expected the next large detachment of them.

" Have you a letter of introduction ? " asked the agent.

" I shouldn't have thought any was necessary," I answered. " A Russian friend advised me to go to you. You don't stand to lose anything by telling me what I want to know."

He would do nothing for me without an introduction, without knowing exactly with whom he had to deal. I might be a political spy. The hand of the Tsar was long, and could ruin men's lives even in America. At least so he thought.

I mentioned the name of a revolutionary anarchist, a militant suffragette. He said a letter from her would suffice. I went to Hampstead and explained my predicament to the lady. She wrote me a note to a mysterious revolutionary who was living above Israel's shop, and this missive, when presented, was promptly taken as a full credential. The mysterious revolutionary was on the point of death, and could not see me, but Israel read the letter, and at once agreed that he was ready to be of any service to me he could. There was a large party of Russians coming soon, not Russian Jews, but real Russian peasants, and he would let me know as soon as he could just when they might be expected. I returned to my ordinary avocations, and every now and then rang up " I. K." on the telephone, and asked, Had the Russians come ? When were they coming ? At last the intelligence came, " They are just arriving. Hurry down to Hayes wharf at once."

The news took me in the midst of other things, but I dropped all and rushed to London Bridge. There, at Tooley Street, I witnessed one of the happenings you'd never think was going on in London.

A long procession of Russian peasants was just filing out from the miserable steamship *Perm*. They were in black, white, and brown sheepskins and in astrakhan hats, some in blue blouses and peak-hats, some in brightly embroidered linen shirts ; none wore collars, but some had new shiny bowlers, on which the litter and dust of the port was continually falling,—bowlers which they had evidently purchased from German hawkers who had come on board at some point in the journey. The women wore sheepskins also, many of them, and their heads were covered with shawls ; they had their babies sewn up in little red quilts. Beside them there were pretty town girls and Jewesses dressed in cottons and serges and cheap hats. There were few old people and many young ones, and they carried under their arms clumsy, red-painted wooden boxes and baskets from which kettles and saucepans dangled. On their backs they had sacks, and in their hands several of them had crusts of bread picked up in their hurry as they were hustled from their berths and through the mess-room. Some of the sacks on their backs, as I afterward saw, contained nothing but crusts of white and black bread, on which, perhaps, they trusted to live during the first weeks in America !

They were all rather bewildered for the moment, and a trifle anxious about the Customs officers.

" What is this town ? " they asked.

" For what are the Customs men looking ? "

" Where is our agent—the man they said would be here ? "

I entered into conversation with them, and over and over again answered the question, " What is this town ? " I told them it was London.

" Is it a beautiful town ? " they asked.

" Is it a large town ? "

" Do we have to go in a train ? "

" How far is it ? "

" Look at my ticket ; what does it say ? "

They made a miscellaneous crowd on the quayside, and

I talked to them freely, answered their questions, and in turn put questions of my own. They came from all parts of Russia, even from remote parts, and were going to just as diverse places in America : to villages in Minnesota, in Michigan, in Iowa ; to Brooklyn, to Boston, to Chicago. I realised the meaning of the phrase, " The magic word Chicago." I told them how many people there were in London, how much dock labourers get a week, pointed out the Tower Bridge, and calmed them about the non-appearance of their agent. I knew him, and if he didn't turn up I would lead them to him. They might be calm ; he knew Russian, he would arrange all for them.

At last a representative of my East End friend appeared —David the Jew. He was known to all the dockers as David, but he had a gilt I. K. on the collar of his coat, wore a collar, had his hair brushed, and was a person of tremendous importance to the eager and humble emigrants. Not a Jew, no ! No Jew has authority in Russia. No Jew looked like David, and so the patient Christians thought him an important official when he rated them, and shouted to them, and cursed them like a herdsman driving home a contrary lot of cows and sheep and pigs.

Another Jew appeared, in a green hat and fancy waistcoat, and he produced a sheaf of papers having the names, ages, and destinations of the emigrants all tabulated. He began a roll-call in one of the empty warehouses of the dock. Each peasant as his name was called was ticked off, and was allowed to gather up his belongings and bolt through the warehouse as if to catch a train. I ran to the other side and found a series of vans and brakes, such as take the East-enders to Happy Hampstead on a Bank Holiday. Into these the emigrants were guided, and they took their seats with great satisfaction. They clambered in from all sides, showing a preference for getting up by the wheels, and nearly pulling away the sides of the frail vehicles.

The vanmen jested after their knowledge of jests, and put their arms round the pretty girls' waists. David rushed to and fro, fretting and scolding. Loafers and clerks collected to look at the girls.

" Why does that old man look at us so ? He ought to be ashamed of himself," said a pretty Moscow girl to me. " He is dressed like twenty or twenty-five, but he is quite old. How quizzically he looks at us."

" He is forty," said I.

" Sixty ! "

" That's a pretty one," said a young man whose firm imported Koslof eggs.

" What does he say ? "

" He says that you are pretty."

" Tell him I thank him for the compliment ; but he is not interesting—he has not a moustache."

All the vans filled, and there was a noise and a smell of Russia in the grim and dreary dockyard, and such a chatter of young men and women, all very excited. At last David got them all in order. I stepped up myself, and one by one we went off through the East End of the city.

We went to St. Pancras station. On the way one of the peasants stepped down from his brake and, entering a Jewish hat-shop, bought himself a soft green felt and put his astrakhan hat away in his sack. He was the subject of some mirth, and also of some envy in the crowd that sat down to coffee and bread and butter at the Great Midland terminus. Under the terms of their tickets the emigrants were fed all the way from Libau to New York without extra charge.

They were all going from Liverpool, some by the Allan Line, some by the White Star, and others by the Cunard.

As by far the greatest number were going on the Cunard boat, I went to I. K. and booked a passage on that line. There was much to arrange and write, my sack to pack, and many good-byes to utter—all in the briefest space of time.

At midnight I returned to the station and took my seat in the last train for Liverpool. Till the moment before departure I had a compartment to myself; but away down at the back of the train were coach after coach of Russians, all stretched on their sheepskins on the narrow seats and on the floor, with their children in the string cradles of the parcel-racks. They were crowded with bundles and baskets and kettles and saucepans, and yet they had disposed themselves to sleep. As I walked along the corridor I heard the chorus of heavy breathing and snoring. In one of the end carriages a woman was on her knees praying—prostrating and crossing herself. As we moved out of St. Pancras I felt as I did when upon the pilgrim boat going to Jerusalem, and I said to myself with a thrill, " We have mysterious passengers on board." The sleeping Russians gave an atmosphere to the English train. It was like the peculiar feeling that comes to the other people in a house when news is given downstairs that a new baby has arrived.

A man stepped into my compartment just as the train was moving—a jovial Briton who asked me to have a cigar, and said, when I refused, that he was glad, for he really wanted to give it to the guard. He wanted the guard to stop the express for him at Wellingborough, and reckoned that the cigar would put him on friendly terms. He inquired whether I was a Mason, and when I said I was not, proceeded to reveal Masonic secrets, unbuttoning his waistcoat to show me a little golden sphere which opened to make a cross.

At St. Albans he gave the guard the cigar, and the charm

worked, for he was enabled to alight at Wellingborough. And I was left alone with my dreams.

In a thunderstorm, with a high gale and showers of blinding hail and snow, with occasional flashing forth of amazing sunshine, to be followed by deepest gloom of threatening cloud, we collected on the quay at Liverpool—English, Russians, Jews, Germans, Swedes, Finns—all staring at one another curiously, and trying to understand languages we had never heard before. Three hundred yards out in the harbour stood the red-funnelled Cunarder which was to bear us to America; and we waited impatiently for the boat which should take us alongside. We carried baskets and portmanteaus in our strained hands; most of us were wearing heavy cloaks, and some had sacks upon their backs, so we were all very ready to rush aboard the ferry-boat and dump our burdens on its damp decks. What a stampede there was—people pushing into portmanteaus, baskets pushing into people! At last we had all crossed the little gangway, and all that remained on shore were the few relatives and friends who had come to see the English off. This pathetic little crowd sang ragtime songs, waved their hats and handkerchiefs, and shouted. There was a bandying of farewells:

" Ta-ta, ta-ta-ta ! "

" Wish you luck ! "

" Ta-ta-a, ole Lloyd George ! No more stamp-licking ! "

" Good luck, old boy ! "

" The last of old England ! "

The foreign people looked on and smiled non-comprehendingly; the English and Americans huzzaed and grinned. Then away we went over the water, and thoughts of England passed rapidly away in the interest of coming nearer to civilisation's toy, the great liner. We felt the romance of ocean travel, and also the tremulous fear which the ocean inspires. Then as we lay in the lee of the vast, steep, blood-and soot-coloured liner, each one of us thought of the *Titanic* and the third-class passengers who went down beneath her into the abyss.

The vastness of the liner made our ferry-boat look like a matchbox. A door opened in the great red wall and a little gangway came out of it like a tongue coming out of a mouth. We all picked up our bags and baggage and pushed and squirmed along this narrow footway that led into the mouth of the steamer and away down into its vast, cavernous, hungry stomach : English, Russians, Jews, Germans, Poles, Swedes, Finns, Flemings, Spaniards, Italians, Canadians, passed along and disappeared — among them all, I, myself.

There were fifteen hundred of us ; each man and woman, still carrying handbags and baskets, filed past a doctor and two assistants, and was cursorily examined for diseases of the eye or skin.

" Hats and gloves off ! " was our first greeting on the liner. We marched slowly up to the medical trio, and each one as he passed had his eyelid seized by the doctor and turned inside out with a little instrument. It was a strange liberty to take with one's person ; but doctors are getting their own way nowadays, and they were looking for *trachoma*. For the rest the passing of hands through our hair and examination of our skin for signs of scabies was not so rough, and the cleaner-looking people were not molested.

Still carrying our things we took our medical-inspection cards and had them stamped by a young man on duty for that purpose. Then we were shown our berths.

There was a spring bed for each person, a towel, a bar of soap, and a life-preserver. The berths were arranged, two, four, and six in a cabin. Married couples could have a room to themselves, but for the rest men and women were kept in different sets of cabins. British were put together, Scandinavians together, Russians and Jews together. It was so arranged that the people in the cabins understood one another's language. Notices on the walls warned that all emigrants would be vaccinated on deck, whether they had been vaccinated before or not ; that all couples making love too warmly would be married compulsorily at New York if the authorities deemed it fit, or should be fined or imprisoned ; that in case of fire or smoke being seen any-where we were to report to chief steward, but not to our fellow-passengers ; that smoking was not allowed except on the upper deck, and so on. The cabins were a glittering, shining white ; they were small and box-like ; they pos-sessed wash-basins and water for the first day of the voyage, but not to be replenished on succeeding days. There were general lavatories where you might wash in hot or cold water, and there were bathrooms which were locked and never used. Each cabin had a little mirror. The cabins were steam-heated, and when the passengers were dirty the air was foul. Fresh air was to be found on the fore and after decks, except in time of storm, when we were barred down. In time of storm the smell below was necessarily worse—atrocious, for most of the people were very sick. We had, however, a great quantity of dark space to our-selves, and could prowl into the most lonesome parts of the vessel. The dark recesses were always occupied by spoon-ing couples who looked as if they had embarked on this journey only to make love to one another. There were parts of the ship wholly given over to dancing, other parts to horse-play and feats of strength. There was an immense dining-room with ante-chambers, and there, to the sound of the jangling dinner-bell echoing and wandering far or near over the ship, we assembled to meals.

The emigrants flocked into the mess-room from the four doors to twenty immense tables spread with knives and forks and toppling platters of bread. Nearly all the men came in in their hats,—in black glistening ringlety sheep-skin hats, in fur caps, in bowlers, in sombreros, in felt hats with high crowns, in Austrian cloth hats, in caps so green that the wearer could only be Irish. Most of the young men were curious to see what girls there were on board, and looked eagerly to the daintily clad Swedish women, blonde and auburn-haired beauties in tight-fitting, speckless jerseys. The British girls came in in their poor cotton dresses, or old silk ones, things that had once looked grand for Sunday wear but now bore miserable crippled hooks and eyes, threadbare seams, gaping fastenings—cheerful daughters of John Bull trapesing along in the shabbiest of floppy old boots. Then there were the dark and somewhat forward Jewesses, talk-ing animatedly with little Jew men in queer-shaped trousers and skimpy coats ; there were slatternly looking Italian women with their children, intent on being at home in whatever circumstances. There was a party of shapely and attractive Austrian girls that attracted attention from the others and a regular scramble to try to sit next to them or near them. No one ever saw a greater miscellaneity and promiscuity of peoples brought together by accident. I sat between a sheepskin-wrapped peasant wife from the depths of Russia and a neat Danish engineer, who looked no different from British or American. Opposite me were two cowboys going back to the Far West, a dandified Span-ish Jew sat next them on one hand and two Norwegians in voluminous knitted jackets on the other. At the next table was a row of boisterous Flemings, with huge caps and gaudy scarfs. There were Americans, spruce and smart and polite ; there were Italians, swarthy and dirty, having their black felt hats on their heads all through the meal and resting their elbows on the table as if they'd just come into a public-house in their native land.   There were gentle youths in shirts which women-folk had embroidered in Little Russia ; there were black-bearded Jewish patriarchs in their gaberdines, tall and gaunt.

A strange gathering of seekers, despairers, wanderers, pioneers, criminals, scapegoats.   I thought of all the reasons that had brought these various folk together to make a community, that had brought them all together to form a Little America.   From Great Britain it is so often the drunkard who is sent.   Some young fellow turns out to be wilder than the rest of his family ; he won't settle down to the sober, righteous, and godly life that has been the destiny of the others ; he is likely to disgrace respectability, so parents or friends give him his passage-money and a little capital and send him away across the sea.   Henceforth his name is mentioned at home with a 'ssh, or with a tear— till the day that he makes his fortune.   With the drunkard go the young forger or embezzler whose shame has been covered up and hidden, but who can get no " character " from his last employer.   Then there are the unemployed, and those discontented with their jobs, the out-of-works, the men who have seen no prospect in the old land and felt no freedom.   There are the wanderers, the rovers, the wastrels, so called, who have never been able to settle down ; there are also the prudent and thoughtful men who have read of better conditions and go simply to take advantage of them.   There are those who are there almost against their will, persuaded by the agents of the shipping companies and the various people interested to keep up the flow of people into America.   There are the women who are going out to their sweethearts to be married, and the wives who are going to the husbands who have " made good " ; there are the girls who have got into trouble at

home and have slid away to America to hide their shame ;
there are girls going to be domestic servants, and girls
doomed to walk the streets,—all sitting down together,
equals, at a table where no grace is said but the whisper of
hope which rises from each heart.

But it is not only just these people whom I have so
materially and separately indicated. The cheerful lad
who is beginning to flirt with his first girl acquaintance on
the boat has only a few hours since dried the tears off his
cheeks ; they are nearly all young people on the boat, and
they mostly have loving mothers and fathers in the background, and friends and sweethearts, some of them. And
there are some lonely ones who have none who care for
them in all the world. There are young men who are following a lucky star, and who will never be so poor again
in their lives, boys who have guardian angels who will
never let them injure their foot on the ground, boys who
have in their favour good fairies, boys and girls who have
old folk praying for them. And there is the prodigal
son, as well as the too-prodigal daughter. There are
youngest brothers in plenty, going to win the princess
in a way their elder brothers never thought of ; young
Hans is there, Aladdin, Norwegian Ashepattle, Ivan Durak
—the Angel of Life is there ; there is also the Angel of
Death.

We sat down together to our first meal,—the whole company of the emigrant passengers broke bread together and
became thereby one body,—a little American nation in
ourselves. I am sure that had the rest of the world's people
been lost we could have run a civilisation by ourselves.
We had peasants to till the soil, colliers to give us fuel,
weavers and spinners to make cloth, tailors to sew it into
garments, comely girls of all nations to be our wives ; we
had clerks and shop-keepers and Jews with which to make

cities ; musicians and music-hall artists to divert us, and an author to write about it all.

Mugs half-full of celery soup were whisked along the tables ; not a chunk of bread on the platters was less than an inch thick ; the hash of gristly beef and warm potato was what would not have been tolerated in the poorest restaurant, but we set ourselves to eat it, knowing that trials in plenty awaited us and that the time might come when we should have worse things than these to bear. The Swedes and the British were finicky ; the Russians and the Jews ate voraciously as if they'd never seen anything so good in their lives.

The peasant woman next to me crossed herself before and after the meal ; her Russian compatriots removed their hats, and some of them said grace in a whisper to themselves. But most ate even with their hats on, and most with their hands dirty. You would not say we ate as if in the presence of God and with the memories, in the mind, of prayers for the future and heart-break at parting with home ; yet this meal was for the seeing eye a wonderful religious ceremony, a very real first communion service. The rough food so roughly dispensed was the bread and wine, making them all of one body and of one spirit in America. Henceforth all these people will come nearer and nearer to one another, and drift farther and farther from the old nations to which they belonged. They will marry one another, British and Jewish, Swedish and Irish, Russian and German ; they will be always eating at America's board ; they will be speaking the one language, their children will learn America's ideals in America's school. Even from the most aboriginal, illiterate peasant on board, there must come one day a little child, his grandson or great-grandson, who will have forgotten the old country and the old customs, whose heart will thrill to America's idea as if he had himself begotten it.

On Sunday morning when we came upstairs from our
stuffy little cabin we were gliding past the green coast of
Ireland, and shortly after breakfast-time we entered the
beautiful harbour of Queenstown, blue-green, gleaming,
and perfect under a bright spring sun. Hawkers came
aboard with apples, knotted sticks, and green favours—
the day following would be St. Patrick's. And we shipped
a score of Irish passengers.

Outside Queenstown a different weather raged over the
Atlantic, and as we steamed out of the lagoon it came forward to meet us. The clouds came drifting toward us, and
the wind rattled in the masts. The ocean was full of glorious life and wash of wave and sea. A crowd of emigrants
stood in the aft and watched the surf thundering away
behind us; the great hillsides of green water rose into
being and then fell out of being in grand prodigality. Gulls
hung over us as we rushed forward and poised themselves
with gentle feet outstretched, or flew about us, skirling and
crying, or went forward and overtook us. Meanwhile Ireland and Britain passed out of view, and we were left alone
with the wide ocean. We knew that for a week we should
not see land again, and when we did see land that land
would be America.

Then we all began to know one another, to talk, to dance,
to sing, to play together. All the cabins were abuzz with
chatter, and along the decks young couples began to find
one another out and to walk arm in arm. Two dreamy
Norwegians produced concertinas, and without persuasion
sat down in dark corners and played dance music for hours,
for days. Rough men danced with one another, and the
more fortunate danced with the girls, dance after dance,
endlessly. The buffets were crowded with navvies clamour-
ing for beer ; the smoking-rooms were full of excited

gamblers thumbing filthy cards. The first deck was wholly in electric light, you mounted to the second and it was all in shadow, you went higher still and you came to daylight. You could spend your waking hours on any of these levels, but the lower you went the warmer it was. On the electric-light deck were to be found the cleaner and more respectable passengers; they sat and talked in the mess-room, played the piano, sang songs. Up above them all the hooligans rushed about, and there also, in the shadow, in the many recesses and dark empty corners young men and women were making love, looking moonily at one another, kissing furtively and giving by suggestion an unwonted atmosphere to the ship. It was also on this deck that the wild couples danced and the card-players shuffled and dealt. Up on the open deck were the sad people, and those who loved to pace to and fro to the march music of the racing steamer and the breaking waves.

I wandered from deck to deck, everywhere; opened many doors, peered into many faces, sat at the card-table, crushed my way into the bar, entered into the mob of dancers, found a Russian girl and talked to her. But I was soon much sought for. When the Russian-speaking people found out I had their language they followed me everywhere, asking elementary questions about life and work and wages in America. Even after I had gone to bed and was fast asleep my cabin door would open and some woolly-faced Little Russian would cry out, "Gospodin Graham, forgive me, please, I have a little prayer to make you; write me also a letter to a farmer."

I had written for several of them notes which they might present at their journey's end.

All day long I was in converse with Russians, Poles, Jews, Georgians, Lithuanians, Finns.

"Look at these Russian fatheads (*duraki*)," said a young

Jew. " Why do they go to America ? Why do they leave their native land to go to a country where they will be exploited by every one ? "

" Why do *you* leave it, then ? " asked a Russian.

" Because I have no rights there," replied the Jew.

" Have we rights ? " the Russian retorted.

" If I had your rights in Russia I'd never leave that country. I'd find something to do that would make me richer than I could ever be in America."

There were three or four peasants around, and another rejoined, " But you could have our rights if you wished."

Whereupon I broke in :

" But only by renouncing the Jewish faith."

" That is exactly the truth," said the Jew.

" Yes," said a Russian called Alexy Mitrophanovitch, " he can have all our rights if he renounces his faith."

" If I am baptized to get your rights what use is that to you ? Why do Christians ask for such an empty thing ? "

" All the same," said another Russian, " in going to America you will break your faith, and so will we. I have heard how it happens. They don't keep the Saints' days there."

Alexy Mitrophanovitch was a fine, tall, healthy-looking peasant workman in a black sheepskin. With him, and as an inseparable, walked a broad-faced Gorky-like tramp in a dusty peak-hat. The latter was called Yoosha.

" You see all I've got," said Alexy to me, " is just what I stand up in. Not a copeck of my own in my pocket, and not a basket of clothes. My friend Yoosha is lending me eighty roubles so as to pass the officials at New York, but of course I give it back to him when we pass the barrier. We worked together at Astrakhan."

" Have you a bride in Russia ? "

No, he was alone. He did not think to marry ; but he

had a father and a mother. At Astrakhan he had been three thousand versts away from his village home, so he wouldn't be so much farther away in America.

He was going to a village in Wisconsin. A mate of his had written that work was good there, and he and Yoosha had decided to go. They would seek the same farmer, a German, Mr. Joseph Stamb—would I perhaps write a letter in English to Mr. Stamb ? . . .

Both he and Yoosha took communion before leaving Astrakhan. I asked Alexy whether he thought he was going to break his faith as the other Russians had said to the Jew. How was he going to live without his Tsar and his Church ?

He struck his breast and said, " There, that is where my Church is ! However far away I go I am no farther from God ! "

Would he go back to Russia ?

He would like to go back to die there.

" Tell me," said he, " do they burn dead bodies in America ? I would not like my body to be burned. It was made of earth, and should return to the earth."

The man who slept parallel with me in my cabin was an English collier from the North Country. He had been a bad boy in the old country, and his father had helped him off to America. Whenever he had a chance to talk to me, it was of whippet-racing and ledgers and prizes and his pet dog.

" As soon as a get tha monny a'll enter that dawg aht Sheffield. A took 'er to Durby ; they wawn't look at 'er there. There is no dawg's can stan' agin her. At Durby they run the rabbits in the dusk, an' the little dawg as 'ad the start could see 'em, but ourn moight a been at Bradford fur all she could see. A'll bet yer that dawg's either dead or run away. She fair lived fer me. Every night she slep'

in my bed. Ef ah locked 'er aht, she kick up such a ra.
Then I open the door an' she'd come straight an' jump into
bed an' snuggle 'erself up an' fall asleep. . . ."

The dirtiest cabins in the ship were allotted to the Russians and the Jews, and down there at nine at night the
Slavs were saying their prayers whilst just above them we
British were singing comic songs or listening to them. Most
of us, I reckon, also said our prayers later on, quietly, under
our sheets ; for we were, below the surface, very solitary,
very apprehensive, very child-like, very much in need of
the comfort of an all-seeing Father.

The weather was stormy, and the boat lost thirty-six
hours on the way over. The skies were mostly grey, the
wind swept the vessel, and the sea deluged her. The storm
on the third night considerably reduced the gaiety of the
ship ; all night long we rolled to and fro, listening to the
crash of the waves and the chorus of the spring mat-
tresses creaking in all the cabins. My boy who had left
the " dawg " behind him got badly " queered up." He
said it was " mackerel as done it," a certain warm, evil-
looking mackerel that had been served him for tea on the
Tuesday evening. Indeed the food served us was not of a
sort calculated to prepare us for an Atlantic storm—roast
corned beef, sausage and mash, dubious eggs, tea that tasted
strongly of soda, promiscuously poked melting butter,
ice cream. On tumultuous Tuesday the last thing we ate
was ice cream ! We all felt pretty abject on Wednesday
morning.

Our sickness was the stewards' opportunity. They inter-
viewed us, sold us bovril and hawked plates of decent ham
and eggs, obtained from the second-class table or their own
mess. The British found the journey hard to bear, though
they didn't suffer so much as the Poles and the Austrians
and the Russians. I found the whole journey compara-

tively comfortable, stormy weather having no effect on me, and this being neither my first nor worst voyage. Any one who has travelled with the Russian pilgrims from Constantinople to Jaffa in bad weather has nothing to fear from any shipboard horror on a Cunarder on the Atlantic.

Only two of the Russians went through the storm happily, Alexy and Yoosha. They had worked for nights and months on the Caspian Sea in a little boat, almost capsizing each moment as they strained at their draughts of salmon and sturgeon ; one moment deep down among the seas, the next plunging upward, shooting over the waves, stopping short, slithering round—as they graphically described it to me.

When the storm subsided the pale and convalescent emigrants came upstairs to get sea air and save themselves from further illness. Corpse-like women lay on the park seats, on the coiled rope, on the stairs, uttering not a word, scarcely interested to exist. Other women were being walked up and down by their young men. A patriarchal Jew, very tall and gaunt, hauled along a small, fat woman of his race, and made her walk up and down with him for her health—a funny pair they looked. On Wednesday afternoon, about the time the sun came out, one of the boisterous Flemings tied a long string to a tape that was hanging under a pretty French girl's skirts, and he pulled a little and watched her face, pulled a little more and watched the trouble, pulled a little more and was found out. Then several of the corpse-like ones smiled, and interest in life was seen to be reviving.

Next morning when I was up forward with my kodak, one of the young ladies who had been so ill was being tossed in a blanket with a young Irish lad of whom she was fond, struggling and scratching and rolling with a young fellow who was kissing her, whilst four companions were dangerously hoisting them shoulder high, laughing and bandying

Irish remarks.   Life only hides itself when these folk are
ill; they will survive more than sea-sickness.

The white dawn is haggard behind us over the black
waves, and our great strong boat goes thundering away
ahead of the sun.   It is mid-Atlantic, and we stare into
the same great circle of hungry emptiness as did Columbus
and his mariners.   Our gaze yearns for land, but finds
none ; it rests sadly on the solitary places of the ocean, on
the forlorn waves lifting themselves far away, falling into
nothingness, and then wandering to rebirth.

Nothing is happening in the wide ocean.   The minutes
add themselves, and become hours.   We know ourselves
far from home, and we cannot say how far from the goal,
but still very far, and there is no turning back.   "Would
there were," says the foolish heart.   "Would I had never
come away from the warm homè, the mother's love, the
friends who care for me, the woman who loves me, the girl
who has such a lot of empty time on her hands now that I
have gone away, her lover."   How lonely it is on the steerage deck in the crowd of a thousand strangers, hearing a
score of unknown tongues about your ears, hearing your
own language so pronounced you scarce recognise it !

The mirth of others is almost unpardonable, the romping
of Flemish boys, pushing people right and left in a break-
neck game of touch; the excitement of a group of Russians
doing feats of strength ; the sweet happiness of dainty
Swedish girls dancing with their rough partners to the
strains of an accordion.   How good to escape from it all
and trespass on the steward's promenade at the very extremity of the after-deck, where the emigrants may not go,
and where they are out of sight and out of hearing.

The ocean is retreating behind us with storm-scud and
smoke of foam threshed out from our riven road.   Vast

theatres of waves are falling away behind us and slipping out of our ken backward into the homeward horizon. Above us the sky is grey, and the sea also is grey, waving now and then a miserable flag of green.

What an empty ocean! There is nothing happening in it but our ship. And for me, that ship is just part of my own purpose : there is nothing happening but what I willed. The slanting red funnels are full of purpose, and the volumes of smoke that fly backward are like our sighs, regrets, hopes, despairs, the outward sign of the fire that is driving us on.

Up on the steward's promenade on Thursday morning I fell into conversation with a young Englishman, and he poured out his heart to me. He was very homesick, and had spoken to no one up till then. He was in a long cloak, with the collar turned up, and a large cloth cap was stuck tightly on his head to keep it from the wind. His face was red with health, but his forehead was puckered, and his eyes seemed ready to shed tears.

" Never been so far away from the old country before ? " I hazarded.

" No."

" Would you like to go back ? "

" No."

" Are you going to friends in America ? "

He shook his head.

" I'm going on my own."

" You are the sort that America wants," I ventured. He did not reply, and I was about to walk away, snubbed, when another thought occurred to me.

" I once left the old country to seek my fortune elsewhere," said I. " I felt as you do, I expect. But it was to go to Russia."

He looked up at me with an inquisitive grimace. I suggested that I knew what it was to part with a girl I loved, and a mother and friends and comforts, and to go to a strange country where I knew no one, and thought I had no friends. At the mention of parting with the girl he seemed to freeze, but curiosity tempted him and he let me tell him some of my story.

" I reckon that England's pretty well played out," said he.

" Not whilst it sends its sons out into the world—you to America, and me to Russia," said I with a smile. " It will only be played out when we haven't the courage to go."

" Well," said he, " I reckon I *had* to go, there wasn't anything else for me to do. It wasn't courage on my part. I didn't want to go. I reckon there ought to be room in England for the likes of me. It isn't as if I had no guts. I'm as fit as they make them, only no good at figures. I think I had the right to a place in England and a decent screw, and England might be proud of me. I should always have been ready to fight against the Germans for her. I joined the Territorials, I learned to shoot, I can ride a horse."

" Why didn't you go into the army ? "

" That's not the place for a decent fellow. Besides, my people wouldn't allow it, and my girl's folks would be cut up. And I reckon there's something better to do than be drilled and wait for a war. My people wanted me to be something respectable, to go into the Civil Service, or a bank, or an insurance office, or even into the wholesale fruit business. I was put into Jacob's, the fruit firm, but I couldn't work their rate. I've been hunting for work the last five months. That takes it out of you, don't it ? How mean I felt ! Everybody looked at me in such a way—

you know, as much as to say ' You loafer, you lout, you good-for-nothing,' so that I jolly well began to feel I was that, too, especially when my clothes got shabby and I had nothing decent to put on to see people."

As my acquaintance talked he rapidly became simpler, more child-like, confiding, and tears stole down his cheek. The reserved and surly lad became a boy. " What a life," said he, " to search work all day, beg a shilling or so from my mother in the evening, meet my girl, tell her all that's happened, then at night to finish the day lying in bed trying to imagine what I'd do if I had a thousand a year !

" I reckon I could have earned a living with my hands, but my people were too proud ; yes, and I was too proud also, and my girl might not have liked it. Still, I'd have done anything to earn a sovereign and take her to the theatre, or go out with her to the country for a day, or make her a nice present and prove I wasn't mean. I used to be generous. When I had a job I gave plenty of presents ; but you can't give things away when you have to borrow each day. You even walk instead of taking a car, and you are mean, mean, mean—mean all day. Then in the evening you talk of marrying a girl, of having a little home, and you dare to kiss her as much as you can or she will let, and all the while you have in the wide world only a few coppers —and a mother."

We went and leaned over the ship and stared down at the sea.

Tears ! I suppose millions had come there before and made that great salt ocean of them.

The boy now lisped his confidence to me hurriedly, happily, tenderly.

" But I reckon I've got a good mother, eh ? She loved me more than I dreamed. How she cried on Friday ! how she cried ! It was wild. Sometimes I used to say I hated

her. I used to shout out angrily at her that I'd run away
and never come back. That was when she said hasty things
to me, or when she wouldn't give me money. I used to
think I'd go and be a tramp, and pick up a living here
and there in the country, and live on fruit and birds' eggs,
sleeping anywhere. It would be better than feeling so
mean at home. But then, my girl—every night I had to
see her. I felt I could not go away like that, never to
come home with a fortune—never, never to be able to
marry her. Every night she put her arms round my neck
and kissed me, and called me her old soldier, her dear one
—all sorts of sweet things. I reckon we didn't miss one
night all this last year.

"Her father's all right. I had thought he would be
different. I was a bit afraid of what he'd say if he got to
hear. But she told him on her own, and one night she took
me home. They had fixed it up themselves without asking
me, and he was very kind. I told him I wanted a job, and
I thought p'raps he was going to get me one. But no ; he
was a queer sort, rather. ' I'm going to wipe out that story
of yours,' he says. Then he goes to his bureau and writes
a note and puts it in an envelope and addresses it to me.
' Here you are, young man,' says he. I opened the envelope and read one word on a slip of paper—AMERICA.
' Millions have told your story before,' says he, ' and have
had that word given them in answer. You get ready to
go to America ; I'll find you your passage-money and
something to start you off in the new country. You'll do
well ; you'll make good, my boy,' and he slapped me on
the back.

"You bet I felt excited. He saw my mother and told
her his plan. She said she couldn't stand in my way. I
got the *Government Handbook on the United States*, and the
emigration circular. I read up America at the public library.

I wonder I hadn't thought of it before. America is a great country, eh? They look at you differently, I bet, and a strong young man's worth something there. My word, when I come back. . . .

"I wonder if I shall come back or if she'll come out to me. I wonder if her father would let her. I guess he would. . . .

"She loves me. My word, how she loves me! I didn't dream of it before. I used to think the harder you kissed, the more it meant; but she kissed me in a new way, so softly, so differently. She said I was hers, that I would be safe wherever I went in the wide world, and I was never to feel afraid. I've got to do without her now. I reckon no other girl is going to mean much to me."

He looked rather scornfully at a troop of pretty Swedes who had invaded our sanctuary.

"It is queer how sure I feel of good luck because of her and what she did. I feel as if everything must turn my way. Downstairs yesterday they challenged me to play a game of cards, and I won fifty cents; but I felt it was wrong to spend my luck that way. The chap wouldn't play any more; he said I was in a lucky vein. He was quite right. Whatever I turn my hand to, I'm bound to have unexpected good luck. I feel so sure I'm going to get a job, and a real good one, too. I shan't play any more cards this journey."

The sun had come out, and the bright light blazed through our smoke, and I felt that the boy's faith was blazing just that way through his regrets.

The sun crept on and overtook us on his own path, and then at last went down in front of us, far away in the waste of waters.

My acquaintance and I went away to the last meal of the day, to the strangely mixed crowd of prospective Americans at the table, where men sat and ate with their hats on, and where no grace was said. " What matter that they throw the food at us ? " I asked. " We are men with stout hearts in our bosoms ; we are going to a great country, where a great people will look at us with creative eyes, making the beautiful out of the ugly, the big and generous out of the little and mean, the headstone out of the rock that the builders rejected."

After supper I left my friend and went upstairs alone. The weather had changed, and the electric lights of the ship were blazing through the rain, the decks were wet and windswept, and the black smoke our funnels were belching forth went hurrying back into the murky evening sky. The vessel, however, went on.

Downstairs some were dancing, some singing, some writing home laboriously, others gossiping, others lying down to sleep in the little white cabins. There was a satisfaction in hearing the throbbing of the engines and feeling the pulse of the ship. We were idle, we passed the time, but we knew that the ship went on.

Going above once more at nine, I found the rain had passed, the sky was clear and the night full of stars. In the sea rested dim reflections of the stars, like the sad faces we see reflected in our memory several days after we have gone from home. I stood at the vessel's edge and looked far over the glimmering waves to the horizon where the stars were walking on the sea. " What will it be like in America ? " whispered the foolish heart. " What will it be like for him ? " Then sadness came—the long, long thoughts of a boy. I whispered the Russian verse :

> " There is a road to happiness,
> But the way is afar."

And yet, next morning, I saw the Englishman dancing

for hours with a pretty Russian girl from a village near Kiev—Phrosia, the sister of Maxim Holost, a fine boy of eighteen going out to North Dakota. I had noticed the Englishman looking on at the dancing, and then suddenly, to my surprise, at a break in the tinkling of the accordion, he offered his arm to the Russian and took her down the middle as the music resumed. . . .

I was much in demand among the Russians on Friday and Saturday, for they wanted to take the English language by storm at the week-end. I taught Alexy by writing out words for him, and six or seven peasants had copied from him and were busy conning " man," " woman," " farm," " work," " give me," " please," " bread," " meat," " is," " Mister," " show," " and," " how much," " like," " more," " half," " good," " bad," the numbers, and so on. They pronounced these words with willing gusto, and made phrases for themselves, calling out to me :

" Show me worrk, pleez."

" Wer is Meester Stamb ? "

" Khao match eez bread ? "

" Give mee haaf."

Alexy tried his English on one of the waiters at dinner time.

" Littel meet, *littel*, give mee more meet."

The steward grinned appreciatively, and told him to lie down and be quiet.

Maxim and his sister were accompanied by a grizzled peasant of sixty or so, wearing a high sugar-loaf hat slipping back from an aged, wrinkled brow. This was Satiron Federovitch, the only old man on deck. His black cloak, deep lined with wadding, was buttoned up to his throat, and the simplicity of his attire and the elemental lines of his face gave him a look of imperturbable calm. Asked why he was going to America, he said that almost every one else in the village had gone before him. A Russian village had as it were vanished from the Russian countryside and from the Russian map and had transplanted itself to Dakota. Poor old greybeard, he didn't want to go at all, but all his friends and relatives had gone, and he felt he must follow.

Holost told every one how at Libau the officials doubted the genuineness of his passport, and he had to telegraph to his village police, at his own expense, to verify his age and appearance. The authorities didn't relish the idea of such a fine young man being lost by any chance to the army. If only they had as much care for the villages as they have for their legions !

I was up betimes on Saturday morning and watched the vessel glide out of the darkness of night into the dusk of the dawn. The electric light up in the main-mast, the eye of the mast, squinted lividly in the half-light, and the great phantom-like ship seemed as if cut out of shiny-white and blood-red cardboard as it moved forward toward the west. The smoke from the funnels lay in two long streamers to the horizon, and the rising sun made a sooty shadow under it on the gleaming waves. As the night-cloud vanished a great wind sprang up, blowing off America. Old Satiron was coming laboriously upstairs, and he slipped out on to the deck incautiously.

" Gee whizz ! " The mocking American wind caught his astrakhan hat and gave it to the sea. Poor old Satiron, he'll turn up in Dakota with a derby on, perhaps.

Saturday was a day of preparation. We packed our things, we wrote letters to catch the mail, we were medically inspected—some of us were vaccinated. All the girls had to take off their blouses and the young men their coats, and we filed past a doctor and two assistants. One man washed each bare arm with a brush and some acid. The doctor looked and examined. The other assistant stood with lymph and lancet and rapidly jabbed us. The operation was performed at an amazing pace, and was only an unpleasant formality. Many of those who were thus vaccinated got their neighbours to suck out the vaccine directly they returned to their cabins. This was what the boy who had left the dog behind him did. He didn't want blood-poisoning, he said. Nearly all the Russians had been vaccinated five or six times already. In Russia there is much disease and much faith in medicine. In England good drainage, many people not vaccinated, little smallpox ; in Russia, no drains, much vaccination, and much of the dread disease.

On Saturday night there was a concert, at which all the steerage were present, and in which any one who liked took part. But English music-hall songs had all the platform —no foreign musicians participated.

Sunday was Easter Day, and I was up in the dark hours of the morning and saw the dawn. Sunrise showed the clouds in the east, but in north and south and west the other clouds still lay asleep. Up on the after-deck of the great tireless steamer little groups of cloaked and muffled emigrants stood gazing over the now familiar ocean. We knew it was our last day on the ship, and that before the dawn on the morrow we should be at the American shore. How fittingly was it Easter, first day of resurrection, festive day of spring, day of promise and hope, the anniversary of happy days, of first communions !

In the wan east the shadowy wings of gulls were flickering. The blood-red sun was just coming into view, streaked and segmented with blackest cloud. He was striving with night, fighting, and at last gaining the victory. High above the east and the wide circle of glory stood hundreds of attendant cloudlets, arrayed by the sun in robes of lovely tinting, and they fled before him with messages for us. Then, astonishing thing, the sun disappeared entirely into shadow. Night seemed to have gotten the victory. But we knew night could not win.

The sun reappeared almost at once, in resplendent silver, now a rim, in a moment a perfect shield. The shield had for a sign a maiden, and from her bosom a lovely light flooded forth upon the world. We felt that we ourselves, looking at it, were growing in stature in the morning. The light enveloped us—it was divine.

But the victory still waited. All the wavelets of the eastern sea were living in the morning, dancing and mingling, bewildering, baffling, delighting, but the west lay all unconquered, a great black ocean of waves, each edged with signs of foam, as if docketed and numbered. All seemed fixed and rigid in death. The sun disappeared again and reappeared anew, and this time he threw into the world ochre and fire. The wide half-circle of the east steamed an ochreous radiance to the zenith. The sun was pallid against the beauty he had shed ; the lenses of the eye fainted upon the unearthly whiteness. It was hard to look upon the splendid one, but only at that moment might he be seen with the traces of his mystery upon him. Now he was in his grave-clothes, all glistening white, but at noon he would be sitting on the right hand of God.

Easter !

" Will there be any service in the steerage to-day ? "

" No, there will only be service for first and second-class passengers."

" Is that because they need it more than we ? "

There was no answer to that impolite remark. Still it was rather amusing to find that the Church's office was part of the luxury of the first and second class.

The third class played cards and danced and sang and flirted much as usual.   They had need of blessing.

So at night a Baptist preacher organised a prayer-meeting on his own account, and the English-speaking people sang " Onward, Christian soldiers," in a rather half-hearted way at eight o'clock, and " Jesus, lover of my soul, let me to Thy Bosom fly," at nine : and there was a prayer and a sermon.

A few hours after I had lain down to sleep Maxim Holost put his head in at my cabin and cried out :

" America !   Come up and see the lights of America."

And without waiting for me to follow, he rushed away to say the same thing to others, " America !   America ! "

II.

THE ARRIVAL OF THE IMMIGRANT.

THE day of the emigrants' arrival in New York was the nearest earthly likeness to the final Day of Judgment, when we have to prove our fitness to enter Heaven. Our trial might well have been prefaced by a few edifying reminders from a priest.

It was the hardest day since leaving Europe and home. From 5 A.M., when we had breakfast, to three in the afternoon, when we landed at the Battery, we were driven in herds from one place to another, ranged into single files, passed in review before doctors, poked in the eyes by the eye-inspectors, cross-questioned by the pocket-inspectors, vice detectives, and blue-book compilers.

Nobody had slept the night before. Those who approached America for the first time stood on the open deck and stared at the lights of Long Island. Others packed their trunks. Lovers took long adieus and promised to write one another letters. There was a hum of talking in the cabins, a continual pattering of feet in the gangways, a splashing of water in the lavatories where cleanly emigrants were trying to wash their whole bodies at hand-basins. At last the bell rang for breakfast : we made that meal before dawn. When it was finished we all went up on the forward deck to see what America looked like by morning light. A little after six we were all chased to the after-deck and made to file past two detectives and an officer. The detectives eyed us; the officer counted to see that no one was hiding.

At seven o'clock our boat lifted anchor and we glided up the still waters of the harbour. The whole prow was a black mass of passengers staring at the ferry-boats, the distant factories, and sky-scrapers. Every point of vantage was seized, and some scores of emigrants were clinging to the rigging. At length we came into sight of the green-grey statue of Liberty, far away and diminutive at first, but later on, a celestial figure in a blaze of sunlight. An American waved a starry flag in greeting, and some emigrants were disposed to cheer, some shed silent tears. Many, however, did not know what the statue was. I heard one Russian telling another that it was the tomb-stone of Columbus.

We carried our luggage out at eight, and in a pushing crowd prepared to disembark. At 8.30 we were quick-marched out of the ship to the Customs Wharf and there ranged in six or seven long lines. All the officials were running and hustling, shouting out, "Come on!" "Hurry!" "Move along!" and clapping their hands. Our trunks were examined and chalk-marked on the run—no delving for diamonds—and then we were quick-marched further to a waiting ferry-boat. Here for the time being hustle ended. We waited three-quarters of an hour in the seat-less ferry, and every one was anxiously speculating on the coming ordeal of medical and pocket examination. At a quarter to ten we steamed for Ellis Island. We were then marched to another ferry-boat, and expected to be trans-ported somewhere else, but this second vessel was simply a floating waiting-room. We were crushed and almost suffocated upon it. A hot sun beat upon its wooden roof; the windows in the sides were fixed; we could not move an inch from the places where we were awkwardly standing, for the boxes and baskets were so thick about our feet; babies kept crying sadly, and irritated emigrants swore at the sound of them. All were thinking—" Shall I get through?" " Have I enough money?" " Shall I pass the doctor?" and for a whole hour, in the heat and noise and discomfort, we were kept thinking thus. At a quarter-past eleven we were released in detachments. Every twenty minutes each and every passenger picked up his luggage and tried to stampede through with the party, a lucky few would bolt past the officer in charge, and the rest would flood back with heart-broken desperate looks on their faces. Every time they failed to get included in the outgoing party the emigrants seemed to feel that they had lost their chance of a job, or that America was a failure, or their coming there a great mistake. At last, at a quarter-past twelve, it was my turn to rush out and find what Fate and America had in store for me.

Once more it was " Quick march!" and hurrying about with bags and baskets in our hands, we were put into lines. Then we slowly filed up to a doctor who turned our eyelids inside out with a metal instrument. Another doctor scanned faces and hands for skin diseases, and then we carried our ship-inspection cards to an official who stamped them. We passed into the vast hall of judgment, and were classified and put into lines again, this time according to our nationality. It was interesting to observe at the very threshold of the United States the mechanical obsession of the American people. This ranging and guiding and hurrying and sifting was like nothing so much as the screening of coal in a great breaker tower.

It is not good to be like a hurrying, bumping, wandering piece of coal being mechanically guided to the sacks of its type and size, but such is the lot of the immigrant at Ellis Island.

But we had now reached a point in the examination when we could rest. In our new lines we were marched into stalls, and were allowed to sit and look about us, and in comparative ease await the pleasure of officials. The hall of judgment was crowned by two immense American flags. The centre, and indeed the great body of the hall, was filled with immigrants in their stalls, a long series of classified third-class men and women. The walls of the hall were booking-offices, bank counters, inspectors' tables, stools of statisticians. Up above was a visitors' gallery where journalists and the curious might promenade and talk about the melting-pot, and America, " the refuge of the oppressed." Down below, among the clerks' offices, were exits ; one gate led to Freedom and New York, another to quarantine, a third to the railway ferry, a fourth to the hospital and dining-room, to the place where unsuitable emigrants are imprisoned until there is a ship to take them back to their native land.

Somewhere also there was a place where marriages were solemnised. Engaged couples were there made man and wife before landing in New York. I was helping a girl who struggled with a huge basket, and a detective asked me if she were my sweetheart. If I could have said " Yes," as like as not we'd have been married off before we landed. America is extremely solicitous about the welfare of women, especially of poor unmarried women who come to her shores. So many women fall into the clutches of evil directly they land in the New World. The authorities generally refuse to admit a poor friendless girl, though there is a great demand for female labour all over the United States, and it is easy to get a place and earn an honest living.

It was a pathetic sight to see the doubtful men and women pass into the chamber where examination is prolonged, pathetic also to see the Russians and Poles empty their purses, exhibiting to men with good clothes and lasting "jobs" all the money they had in the world.

At half-past two I gave particulars of myself and showed the coin I had, and was passed.

"Have you ever been arrested?" asked the inspector.

Well, yes, I had. I was not disposed to lie. I had been arrested four or five times. In Russia you can't escape that.

"For a crime involving moral turpitude?" he went on.

"No, no."

"Have you got a job in America?" (This is a dangerous question; if you say 'Yes' you probably get sent back home; it is against American law to contract for foreign labour.)

I explained that I was a tramp.

This did not at all please the inspector. He would not accept that definition of my occupation, so he put me down as author.

"Are you an anarchist?"

"No."

"Are you willing to live in subordination to the laws of the United States?"

"Yes."

"Are you a polygamist?"

"What does that mean?" I asked.

"Do you believe a man may possess more than one wife at a time?"

"Certainly not."

"Have you any friends in New York?"

"Acquaintances, yes."

"Give me the address."

I gave him an address.

"How much money have you got?" . . . "Show me, please!" . . . And so on. I was let go.

At three in the afternoon I stood in another ferry-boat, and with a crowd of approved immigrants passed the City of New York. Success had melted most of us, and though we were terribly hungry, we had words and confidences for one another on that ferry-boat. We were ready to help one another to any extent in our power. That is what it feels like to have passed the Last Day and still believe in Heaven, to pass Ellis Island and still believe in America.

Two or three of us hastened to a restaurant. I sat down at a little table and waited. So did the others, but we were making a mistake, for there were no waiters. We had as yet to learn the mechanism of a " Quick Lunch " shop ; there was a certain procedure to be observed and followed, we must learn it if we wanted a dinner. I watched the first American citizen who came in, and did as he did. First I went to the cashier and got a paper slip on which were printed many numbers 5, 10, 15, 25, and so on in intervals of fives. These represented cents, and were so arranged for convenience in adding and for solid profit. At this restaurant nothing cost less than five cents (two-pence halfpenny), and there were no intermediaries between five and ten, ten and fifteen, and so forth. The unit then was five cents, and not as in England two cents (one penny). Obviously this means enormous increase of takings in the long run. That five-cent unit is part of the foundation of American prosperity. I obtained my slip so numbered. Then I took a tray from a stack of trays and a glass from an array of glasses, a fork and a knife from the fork basket, and I went to the roast chicken counter and asked for roast chicken. A plate of hot roast chicken was put on my tray, and the white-hatted cook punched off twenty-five cents on my slip. I went to another counter and received a plate of bread and butter, and to yet another and sprinkled pepper and salt from the general sprinklers. I went and drew iced water. Then, like the slave of the lamp working for himself, I put the whole on my little table. When I had finished my first course I put my plate aside and took my tray to the cook and received a second, and when I had finished that I fetched my coffee.

"Well," thought I, looking round, "no waiters, that means no tips; there is not even a superfluous mendicant boy in charge of the swinging doors." So I began to learn that in America the working man pays no tips.

My companions at the other tables were getting through with their dinners and looking across at one another with congratulatory smiles. We would have sat together, but in this shop one table accommodated one customer only—an unsociable arrangement. I waited for them to finish, so that we could go out together.

Whilst doing so a man came up to me from another table and said very quietly:

"Just come over?"

"This morning," I replied.

He brightened up and asked:

"Looking for a job?"

"You don't mean to say I am being offered one already?" said I.

"That's about it, two dollars."

"Two dollars a day?"

"That's the idea."

"What's the work?"

"Brick-making."

It was brick-making up country for some Trust Company. I said I was staying in New York, couldn't go just yet. He might try my acquaintances. I pointed them out.

One of them, a Pole, said he would go. The contractor

went out with us, and we accompanied him to his office. We took a street car. The fare was five cents, a " nickel," and it was necessary to put the coin in the slot of the conductor's money-box before entering. The conductor stood stiff, like an intelligent bit of machinery, and we were to him fares not humans. The five cents would take me to the other end of the city if I wished it, but there was no two-cent fare in case I wished to go a mile. That five-cent unit again !

We sat in the car and looked out of the windows, interested in every sight and sound. First we had glimpses of the East Side streets, all push-carts and barrows, like Sukhareva at Moscow. Then we saw the dark overhead railway and heard the first thunder of the Elevated train. We went up the Bowery, unlike any other street in the world ; we noted that it was possible to get a room there for twenty cents a night. We stared curiously at the life-sized carved and painted Indians outside the cigar stores, and at the gay red-and-white stripe of the barbers' revolving poles.

We alighted just by a barber's shop. The agent showed us his office and told us to come in if we changed our minds and would like the job. There we left the Pole, and indeed saw him no more.

There were two others beside myself—a Russian and a Russian Jew. As the Jew and I both wanted a shave we all went into the barber's shop. We were still carrying our bags, and were rather a strange party to enter a shop together. But the barbers, a pleasant array of close-shaven smiling Italians, were not put out in the least. They were ready to shave any living thing. Their job was to shave and take the cash, and not to be amused at the appearance of the customers.

In America the barber's shop has a notice outside

stating the number of barbers. If the number is high it is considerable recommendation. Then the briskly revolving pole suggests that it's your turn next and no waiting.

I was put into an immense velvet-bottomed adjustable chair, my legs were steadied on a three-foot stand, and the barber turning a handle caused the back of the chair to collapse gently so that my head and body pointed towards the doorway like the cannon mouth. Then the shave commenced, and the barber twirled my head about and round as if it were on a revolving hinge. And how laborious he was! In America, quick lunch and slow shave; in England quick shave and slow lunch. And fifteen cents for a shave, and thirty-five for a hair-cut.

"That's a high price," said I.

"Union rate," said he. "We are now protected against the public."

The Jew, however, paid five cents less; he had bargained beforehand. He said it was the last cent he'd pay for a shave in that country; he'd buy a safety razor. The Russian smiled; he hadn't shaved yet, and didn't intend to, ever.

At this point the Jew parted company with us. He was going to find a friend of his in Stanton Street. The Russian and I made for a lodging-house in Third Avenue. At a place ticketed "Rooms by the day or month," we rang the bell, rang the bell and waited, rang again. We were to be initiated into another mystery of New York, the mechanical door, the door which has almost an intelligence of its own. Down came a German woman at last, and gave us a rare scolding. Why hadn't we turned the handle and come in? Why had we brought her down so many flights of stairs?

It appeared that by turning a handle in her room on

the second floor she liberated the catch in the lock, and all the visitor had to do was to turn the handle and walk in.

"I heard a rattle in the lock," said I. "I wondered what it meant."

"How long've you been in America?" she asked.

"A few hours. We want rooms for a few days while we look about."

"Days? My lodgers take rooms for years. I haven't any one staying less than six months."

This was just "boosting" her rooms, but I didn't know. I took it for a good sign. If her tenants stayed long terms the place must be very clean. But it was only "boosting." Still the rooms looked decent, and we took them. They were the same price as similar rooms in the centre of London, ten shillings a week, but dearer than in Moscow, where one would pay fifteen roubles (seven and a half dollars or thirty shillings) a month for such accommodation. The floors were carpeted, the sheets were white, there was a good bathroom for each four lodgers, no children, and all was quiet. Laundry was collected, there was no charge for the use of electric light, you received a latch-key on the deposit of twenty-five cents, and could come in any hour of the day or night. In signing the registration book I saw I was the only person of Anglo-Saxon name, all were Germans, Swedes, Italians, Russians. With British caution I hid a twenty-five dollar bill in the binding of one of the most insignificant of my books, so that if I were robbed of the contents of my pocket-book I should still have a stand-by. But my suspicions were begotten only of ignorance. My fellow-lodgers were all hard-working, self-absorbed New Yorkers, who took no thought of their neighbours, either for good or evil.

III.

THE PASSION OF AMERICA AND THE TRADITION OF BRITAIN.

I CAME to America to see men and women and not simply bricks and mortar, to understand a national life rather than to moan over sooty cities and industrial wildernesses. Hundreds of thousands of healthy Europeans passed annually to America. I wanted to know what this asylum or refuge of our wanderers actually was, what was the life and hope it offered, what America was doing with her hands, what she was yearning for with her heart. I wished to know also what was her despair.

On my second day in New York I was deploring the sky-scraper, when a young American lifted her arms above her head in yearning and aspiration saying, " Have you seen the Woolworth Building ? It is a bird's flight of stone right away up into the sky, it is higher and newer than anything else in New York, its cream-coloured walls are pure and undefiled. It is a commercial house, to be let to ten thousand business tenants. But it is like a cathedral ; its foundations are on the earth, but its spire is up among the stars ; if you go to it at sundown and look upward you will see the angels ascending and descending, and hear the murmur of Eternity about it."

I had always thought of the sky-scraper as a black grimy street-front that went up to an unearthly height, a Noah's Ark of sodden and smoky bricks. That is what a sky-scraper would tend to be in London. I had forgotten the drier, cleaner atmosphere of New York.

I went to see the Woolworth Building, and I found it something new. It was beautiful. It was even awe-inspiring.

In the evening I asked an American literary man whom I met at a club what he thought was the *raison d'être* of the Woolworth ; was it not simply the desire to build higher than all other houses—the wish to make a distinct commercial hit ?

He " put me wise."

" First of all," said he, " New York is built on the little island of Manhattan. The island is all built over, and so, as we cannot expand outward we've got to build upward. Ground rent, too, has become so high that we must build high for economy's sake."

I remarked on the number of men who lost their lives in the building of sky-scrapers. " For every minute of the day there was a man injured in some town or other of the United States," so I had read in an evening paper.

He said the Americans were playing large, and must expect to lose a few men in the game. He expected the America of the future would justify all sacrifices made just now, and he gave me in the course of a long talk his view of the passion of America.

" The Woolworth Building is only an inadequate symbol of our faith," said he. " You British and the Germans and French are working on a different principle, you are playing the small game, and playing it well. You stake your efficiency on the perfection of details. In the German life, for instance, nothing is too small to be thought unmeriting of attention."

I told him the watchword of the old chess champion Steinitz, " I do not vant to vin a pawn ; it is enough if I only veakens a pawn."

"You play chess?" said he, laughing. "That's it exactly. He did not care to sacrifice pieces; he was entirely on the defensive in his chess, eh? And in life he would be the same, hoarding his pennies and his dollars, and economising and saving. That's just how the American is different. He doesn't mind taking great risks; he is playing the large game, sacrificing small things, hurrying on, building, destroying, building again, conquering, dreaming. We are always selling out and re-investing. You are concentrating on yourselves as you are; we want to leave our old bodies and conditions behind and jump to a new humanity. If an American youth could inherit the whole world, he would not care to improve it if he saw a chance of selling it to some one and getting something better."

"The spirit of business," I suggested.

"Call it what you will."

"But," said I, "does not this merely result in a town full of a hustling, mannerless crowd; trolley-cars dashing along at life-careless speed; a nation at work with loosely constructed machinery; callous indifference on the part of the living towards those whom they kill in their rush to the goal?"

My new acquaintance looked at me in a way that seemed to say "You—Britisher." He was a great enthusiast for his country, and I had been sent to him by friends in London who wanted me to get to the heart of America, and not simply have my teeth set on edge by the bitter rind.

"You think the end will justify the proceedings?" I added.

"Oh yes," he said. "You know we've only been fifty years on this job; there's nothing in modern America more than fifty years old. Think of what we've done in the time—clearing, building, engineering; think of the bridges we've built, the harbours, the canals, the great factories, the schools. We've been taxed to the last limit of physical strength, and only to put down the pavement and the gas-pipes, so to speak, the things you found ready made for you when you were born, but which we had to lay on the prairie. We are only now beginning to look round and survey the foundations of civilisation. Still most of us are hurrying on, but the end will be worth the trials by the way : we

> " Are whirling from heaven to heaven,
> And less will be lost than won."

" But is it not a miserable, heartless struggle for the individual ? " said I. " For instance, to judge by the story of *The Jungle* I should gather that the lot of a Russian family come fresh to Chicago was terrible."

" Oh, you mustn't take Sinclair literally. He is a Socialist who wants to show that society, as it is at present constituted, is so bad that there is no hope except in revolution. There is heartbreak often, but the struggle is not heartless. It is amazingly full of hope. If you go into the worst of our slums you'll find the people hopeful, even in extremity. I've been across to London, and I never saw such hopeless-looking people as those who live in your East Ham and West Ham and Poplar and the rest of them."

" There is hope with us too," I protested. " The people in our slums are very rebellious : they look forward to the dictatorship of Will Thorne or George Lansbury."

" Ah well," my friend assented, " that's your kind of hope—rebelliousness, hatred of the splendid and safe machine. That's just it. We haven't your rebelliousness and quarrelsomeness. The new-come immigrant is always quarrelling with his neighbours. It is only after a while that America softens him and enriches his heart. The vastness of America, the abundance of its riches is infectious ; it makes the heart larger. The immigrant feels he has room, life is born in him."

"But," said I, "the great machine is here as in Europe. A man is known by his job here just as much as with us, isn't he ? He is labelled and known, he fills a fixed place and has a definite rotation. Every man says to him, 'I see what you are, I know what you are ; you are just what I see and no more.' His neighbour takes him for granted thus. Out of that horrible taking-for-granted springs rebelliousness and hate of the great machine. You must be as rebellious as we are."

"No, no." My companion wouldn't have it. "We don't look at people that way in America. But you're right about looks. It's looks that make people hate. It's eyes that make them curse and swear and hate. Every day hundreds and thousands of eyes look at one. I think eyes have power to create. If thousands and thousands of people pass by a man and look at him with their eyes they almost change him into what they see. If in the course of years millions of eyes look at an individual and see in him just some little bolt in a great machine, then his tender human heart wants to turn into iron. The ego of that man has a forlorn and terrible battle to fight. He thinks he is fighting himself ; he is really fighting the millions of creative eyes who by faith are changing flesh and blood into soulless machinery."

"And here ? " I queried.

He laughed a moment, and then said seriously, "Here it is different. Here we are playing large. Oh, the dwarfing power, the power to make you mean, that the millions of eyes possess in a country that is playing the small game ! They make you feel mean and little, and then you become mean. They kill your heart. Your dead little heart withdraws the human films and the tenderness and imaginativeness from your eyes, and you also begin to look out narrowly, dwarfingly, compellingly. You eye the people in the streets, in the cars, in the office, and they can't help becoming what you are."

" But some escape," said I.

" Yes, some go and smash windows and get sent to gaol, some become tramps, and some come to America. In Giant Despair's dungeon poor Christian exclaims, ' What a fool I am to remain here when I have in my heart a key which I am persuaded will unlock any of the doors of this castle. Strange that it has only now occurred to me that all I need to do is to lift my hand and open the door and go away.' Then poor Christian books a passage to America or Australia. He starts for the New World ; and the moment he puts his foot on the vessel he begins to outgrow. He was his very smallest and meanest under the pressure of the Old World ; when the pressure is removed he begins to expand. He is free. He is on his own. He is sailing to God as himself. The exception has beaten the rule. Now I hold as a personal belief that we are all exceptions, that we take our stand before God as tender human creatures of His, each unique in itself. The emigrant on the boat has the delicious feelings of convalescence, of getting to be himself again. He basks in the sun of freedom. The sun itself seems like the all-merciful Father, the Good Shepherd who cares for each one and knows each by name, leading him out to an earthly paradise."

"That paradise is America, eh ? " said I rather mockingly, and then I paused and added, " But America ought to be really a paradise ; it is pathetic to think of the difference between America as the Russian thinks it to be and America as it is. It is a shame that your trusts and tariffs and corrupt police should have made America a worse place to live in than the Old World. I know it is the land of opportunity, opportunity to become rich, to get on, to be famous; but for the poor immigrant it is rather the land of opportunism, a land where he himself is the opportunity, which not he but other people have the chance to seize."

My friend was scandalised. "I think it gives every one an opportunity," said he, "even the drunkard and the thief and the embezzler whom you so incharitably hand over to us. You know the saying, 'It takes an ocean to receive a muddy stream without defilement.' The ocean of American life cleanses many a muddy stream of the Old World."

"Still," said I, "not to abandon oneself utterly to ideas, is it not true that Pittsburg actually destroys thousands of Slav immigrants yearly? It utterly destroys them. They have no children who come to anything—they are just wiped out. I gather so much from your Government survey of Pittsburg."

"Well," said he, "that survey is just part of the New America, of the new national conscience. Terrible things do happen, witness the enormous white-slave traffic. You have just come to us at the right moment to see the initiation of sweeping changes. President Wilson is like your David Lloyd George, only he has more power, because he has more people at his back. We are just beginning a great progressive era. On the other hand, America is not the place of the weak. That's why we send so many back home from Ellis Island. We've got something else to do than try and put Humpty Dumpty up on the wall again. When the weaker get past Ellis Island into our fierce national life they are bound to go to the wall. We haven't time even to be sorry, and if questioned we can only answer that we believe the sacrifice will be justified."

I recalled to my mind the startling objection of Ivan

Karamazof in the greatest of Russian novels. "When God's providence is fulfilled we shall understand all things; we shall see how the pain and death of, for instance, a little child could be necessary. I understand of course what an upheaval of the universe it will be when everything in heaven and earth blends in one hymn of praise, and everything that lives and has lived cries aloud, 'Thou art just, O Lord, for Thy ways are revealed'; but to my mind the pain of one little child were too high a price to pay." Ivan Karamazof would certainly have renounced the grand future of America bought by the exploitation of thousands of weak and helpless ones.

Still I suppose the past must take care of itself, and the America which stands to-day on the threshold of a new era has more thought and tenderness for the victims of its commercial progress. It is making up its mind to save the foreign women and their little babies. For the rest, America plays large, as my friend said. There is a spaciousness with her, there is contrast, there is life and death, virtue and sin, things to laugh over and things to cry over. The little baby buds are taken away and branches are lopped, but the mustard grows a great tree.

There is a chance in America, a chance that you may be a victim, but also a chance that you may be in at the mating of the King.

.　　　.　　　.　　　.　　　.　　　.

Several months later, when I had tramped some six hundred American miles, and talked to all manner of persons, I realised that America was superlatively a place of hope. I had been continually asking myself, "What *is* America? What *is* this new nation? How are they different from us at home in England?" And one morning, sitting under a bush in Indiana, the answer came to me and I wrote it down. They are fundamentally people who have crossed the Atlantic Ocean, and we are stay-at-homes. They are adventurous, hopeful people. They are people who have thrown themselves on the mercy of God and Nature.

We live in a tradition; they live in an expectation. We are remedying the old state ; they are building the new. We are loyal to the ideas of our predecessors ; they are agape to divine the ideas of generations yet to come.

It is possible to come to Britain and see what Britain is, but if you go to America the utmost you can see is what America is becoming. And when you see the Briton you see a man steadfast at some post of duty, but the American is something to-day but God-knows-what to-morrow. Our noblest epitaph is " He knew his job " ; theirs, " He sacrificed himself to a cause."

Observe, " that state of life unto which it shall please God to call me " puts the Briton in a static order of things. He is in his little shop, or at the forge, or in the coal yard. Within his sight is the Norman tower of the village church. He is known to the priest by his name and his job. He is part of the priests' cure of souls. His life is functionised at the village altar and not at the far shrines of ambition. He belongs to the peasant world. Even though he is English he is as the Russian, " one of God's faithful slaves."

Thousands of English, Scotch, and Irish, simple souls, say their prayers to God each night, not because they are pillars of a chapel or have lately been " saved," but because they have been brought up in that way of life and in that relation to God. They pray God sometimes in anguish that they may be helped *to do their duty*. They say the Lord's Prayer, not as a patter, but with the stark simplicity which you associate with the grey wall of the old church.

These village folk of ours are like old trees. Close your

eyes to the visible and open them to the invisible world, and you see the young man of to-day as the stem, his father as the branch, his grandfather the greater branch. You see in the shadow rising out of the earth the ancient trunk. You think of many people, and yet it is not father and grandfather, and grandfather and great-grandfather, and so on, but one tree, the name of which is the young man leafing in the world of to-day. That man is no shoot, no seedling, he has behind him the consciousness of the vast umbrageous oak. When he says " Our Father, which art in heaven," the voice comes out of the depths of the earth, and it comes from father and grandfather, and from grey-beard after greybeard standing behind one another's shoulders, innumerably.

The place to which it shall please God to call you is not a definite locality in the United States of America ; the dream of wealth is dreamed inside each cottage door. Each man is intent on getting on, on realising something new. He is revolving in his mind ways of doing more business ; of doing what he has more quickly, more economically ; ways of " boosting," ways of buying. Our customers *buy from* us : his customers *trade with* him—they enter into harmony with him. Store-keepers and customers sing together like gnats over the oak trees ; they make things hum. There is a feeling that whether buying or selling you are getting forward.

The British, however, put a great question-mark in front of this American life. Do those who are striving know what they want in the end of ends ? Do those toiling in the wood know what is on the other side ?

The late Price Collier remarked that the German thinks he has done something when he has an idea and the French-man when he has made an epigram ; it may be inferred that the American thinks he has done something when he

3

has made his pile. The ultimate earthly prize for " boosting " and bargaining is a vulgar solatium—a big house, an
abundant person, a few gold rings, an adorned wife, a high-
power touring car.   Out in those wider spaces where lagging
and outdistanced competitors are not taken into your counsel
you still handle business. But now it is in " graft " that
you deal.   You are engineering trusts and cornering com-
modities, you develop political " pull," you own saloons,
and have ledgers full of the bought votes of Italians and
Slavs.

You are great . . . sitting at the steering-wheel of this
great ramshackle political and commercial machine, your
coat off and your immaculate lawn sleeves tucked up above
your elbows ; you own to wolfish-eyed reporters that you
have an enormous appetite for work and zest for life.

And yet . . .

What is the crown ? You die in the midst of it.   There
is no goal, no priceless treasure that even in the death-
struggle your hands grasp after.

Some of your children are going in for a life of pleasure.
They go to be the envy of waiters and hotel-porters and all
people waiting about for tips, but often to be the laughing-
stock of the cultured. One of your sweet but simple-souled
daughters is going to marry a broken-down English peer.
He will not marry her for less than a million dollars.   In
the old store where you began business, gossiping over
bacon and flour, you would have looked rather blank if
some one had said that a foreigner would consent to marry
your daughter only on the payment of an indemnity.

"Well," said my road-companion to me under a bush
in Indiana, " the game goes to pass the time. The world
is a prison-house, and a good game has been invented, commerce, and it saves us from ennui ; that is the philosophy of
it all. Scores of years pass like an hour over cards. Those

who win are most interested and take least stock of the time—and they have invented happiness."

But I cannot believe that the American destiny leads up a cul-de-sac. We have been following out a cross-road. There is a high road somewhere that leads onward.

There are two sorts of immigrant—one that makes his pile and returns to Europe, the other who thinks America a desirable place to settle in. The second class is vastly more numerous than the first, for faith in American life is even greater than faith in America's wealth.

Quite apart from the opportunities for vulgar success America has wonderful promise. It can offer to the new-come colonist a share in a great enterprise. It is quite clear to the sympathetic observer that something is afoot in the land which in Great Britain seems to be best known by police scandals, ugly dances, sentimental novels, and boastful, purse-conscious travellers.

The dream of Progress by which Westerners live is going to be carried forward to some realisation in America. There is a great band of workers united in the idea of making America the most pleasant and happy place to live in that the world has ever known. I refer to those working with such Americans as J. Cotton Dana, the fervent librarian ; Mr. Fred Howe, who is visualising the cities of the future ; the President of the City College, who has such regard not only for the cultural but for the physical well-being of young men ; Jane Addams, who with such precision is diagnosing social evils ; President Wilson, who promises to uproot the tree of corruption ; to mention only the chief of those with whom I was brought in contact in my first experience of America.

The political struggles of America form truly a sad spectacle, but by a thousand non-political signs one is aware that there is a real passion in the breast of the individual.

Going through the public gardens at Newark I see written up : " Citizens, this park is yours. It was planted for you, that the beauty of its flowers and the tender greenery of tree and lawn might refresh you. You will therefore take care of it. . . ."

Going through Albany I find it placarded : " Dirt is the origin of sin ; get rid of dirt, and other evils will go with it," and the whole city is having a clean-up week, all the school children formed into anti-dirt regiments making big bonfires of rubbish and burying the tomato-cans and rusty iron.

Every city in America has been stirring itself to get clean. Even in a remote little place like Clarion, Pa., I read on every lamp-post : " Let your slogan be ' Do it for Home, Sweet Home '—clean up ! " and again in another place, " Develop your social conscience ; you've got one, make the country beautiful." In New York I have handed me the following prayer, which has seemed to me like the breath of the new passion :

We pray for our sisters who are leaving the ancient shelter of the home to earn their wage in the store and shop amid the press of modern life. Grant them strength of body to bear the strain of unremitting toil, and may no present pressure unfit them for the holy duties of home and motherhood which the future may lay upon them. Give them grace to cherish under the new surroundings the old sweetness and gentleness of womanhood, and in the rough mingling of life to keep the purity of their hearts and lives untarnished. Save them from the terrors of utter want. Teach them to stand by their sisters loyally, that by united action they may better their common lot. And to us all grant wisdom and firm determination, that we may not suffer the women of our nation to be drained of strength and hope for the enrichment of a few, lest our homes grow poor in the wifely sweetness and motherly love which have been the saving strength and glory of our country. If it must be so that our women toil like men, help us still to reverence in them the mothers of the future. If they yearn for love, and the sovereign freedom of their own home, give them in due time the fulfilment of their sweet desires. By Mary the beloved, who bore the world's redemption in her bosom ; by the memory of our own dear mothers who kissed our souls awake ; by the little daughters who must soon go out into that world which we are now fashioning for others, we pray that we may deal aright by all women.

Men are praying for women, and women are working for themselves. Commercial rapacity is tempered by women's tears, and the tender stories of the shop-girl that O. Henry wrote are more read to-day than they were in the author's lifetime. The newspapers are all agog with the " vice-probes," scandals, questions of eugenics, the menace of organised capital, the women's movement. And they are not so because vice is more prolific than in Europe, or the race more inclined to fail, or the working men and working women more tyrannised over. They are so because this generation wishes to realise something of the New Jerusalem in its own lifetime. It may be only a foolish dream, but it provides the present atmosphere of America. It discounts the despair which on the one hand prudery and on the other rag-time dancing invite. It discounts the commercial and mechanical obsession of the people. It discounts the wearisome shouting of the cynic who has money in his pocket, and makes America a place in which it is still possible for the simple immigrant to put his trust. In the light of this passion, and never forgetful of it, I view all that comes to my notice in America of to-day.

IV.

INEFFACEABLE MEMORIES OF NEW YORK.

FIRST, the flood of the homeward tide at six-thirty in the evening, the thousands and tens of thousands of smartly dressed shop-girls hurrying and flocking from the lighted West to the shadowy East—their bright, hopeful, almost expectant features, their vivacity and energy even at the end of the long day. I felt the contrast with the London crowd, which is so much gloomier and wearier as it throngs into our Great Eastern terminus of Liverpool Street. New York has a stronger class of girl than London. Our shop-girls are London-bred, but your Sadie and Dulcie are the children 'of foreigners ; they have peasant blood in them and immigrant hope. They have a zest for the life that New York can offer them after shop-hours.

The average wage of the American shop-girl is stated to be seven dollars (twenty-eight shillings) per week ; the average wage in London is about ten shillings, or two and a half dollars.* I suppose that is another reason why our New York sisters are more cheerful. Despite the high price of food in New York there must be a comparatively broad margin left to the American girl to do what she likes with. The cult of the poor little girl of the Department Store is perhaps only a cult. For there are many women in New York more exploited than she. When the shop-girl sells herself to

* In Russia the average wage of the shop-girl is 12 roubles a month (*i.e.* 1½ dollars, or 6s. a week), but then she is a humble creature and lives simply.

rich men for marriage or otherwise she does so because she has been infected by the craze for finery and wealth, is energetic and vivacious, and is morally undermined. It is not because she is worn out and ill-paid. If New York is evil it is not because New York is a failure. The city is prosperous and evil as well. The freshness and health and vigour of the rank and file of New York were amazing to one familiar with the drab and dreary procession of workers filing into the city of London at eight in the morning and away from it at the same hour in the evening.

Then the Grand Central Station, with its vast high hall of marble, surmounted by a blue-green ceiling which, aping heaven itself, is fretted and perforated and painted to represent the clear night sky. That starry roof astonished me. It reminded me of a story I heard of G. K. Chesterton, that he lay in bed on a Sunday morning and with a crayon mounted on a long handle drew pictures on the white ceiling. It was like some dream of Chesterton's realised.

For a long time I looked at the painted roof and picked out my beloved stars and constellations,—the planets under which I like to sleep,—and then I thought, " Strange, that out in the glowing Broadway, not far away, the real stars are hidden from the gaze of New York by flashing and twinkling and changing sky-signs in manifold colour and allurement. Every night the dancing-girl is dancing in the sky, and the hand pours out the yellow beer into the foaming glass which, like the vision of the Grail, appears but to vanish ; every night the steeds prance with the Greek chariot, the athletes box, the kitten plays with the reel. These are the real stars and constellations of Broadway, for Charles's Wain is never seen, neither Orion nor the chair of Cassiopeia nor the Seven Sisters. To see them you must come in here, into the Grand Central Station."

But apart from this paradox, what a station this is—a great silent temple, a place wherein to come to meditate and to pray. It is more beautiful than any of the churches of America. How much more beautiful than the Cathedral of St. John the Divine, for instance. That cathedral will be the largest church in the world when it is finished, and, vanity of vanities, how much more secular it is than the station! It is almost conceivable that, after some revolution in the future, New York might change its mind and go to worship at the Grand Central Station and run its trains into the Cathedral of St. John.

Americans are proud of saying that the Woolworth Building, the Grand Central Station, the Pennsylvania Railway Station, and the New York Central Library show the New York of the future. Almost everything else will be pulled down and built to match these. They are new buildings, they are the soul of the New America finding expression. They are temples of a new religion. Americans pray more and aspire more to God in these than they do in their churches.

.   .   .   .   .   .

There stands out in my memory the East Side, and the slums which I walked night after night in quest of some idea, some redeeming feature, something that would explain them to me. I walked almost at random, taking ever the first turning to the left, the first to the right, and the first to the left again, coming ever and anon to the river and the harbour, and having to turn and change.

The East Side is more spectacular than the East End of London. The houses are so high, and there is so much more crowding, that you get into ten streets of New York what we get into a hundred streets. The New York slums are slums at the intensest. The buildings, great frames of rags and dirt, hang over the busy street below, and are wildly alive from base to summit. All day long the bedding hangs out at the windows or on the iron fire-escapes attached to the houses. Women are shouting and children are crying on the extraordinary stairs which lead from room to room and story to story in the vast honeycomb of dens. On the side-walk is a rough crowd speaking all tongues. The toy doors of the saloons swing to and fro, simple couples sit on high stools in the soda-bars and suck various kinds of " dope." Lithuanian and Polish boys are rushing after one another with toy pistols, the girls are going round and round the barber's pole, singing and playing, with hands joined. The stores are crowded, and notices tell the outsider that he can buy two quarts of Grade B milk for eleven cents, or ten State eggs for twenty-five cents. You come to streets where all the bakers' shops are " panneterias," and you know you are among the Italians. One Hundred and Thirteenth Street as it goes down from Second Avenue to First Avenue is full of Greeks and Italians, and is extraordinarily dark and wild ; men of murderous aspect are prowling about, there is howling across the street from tenement to tenement. Dark, plump women stand at doorways and stare at you, and occasionally a negress in finery trapes past.

You come to little Italian theatres where the price of admission is only five cents, and find them crammed with families, so that you cannot hear *Rigoletto* for the squalling of the babies. There are mean cinema houses where you see only worn-out and spoiled films giving broken and incoherent stories. And all the while the lights and shadows play, the Greek hawker of confectionery shouts :

" Soh-dah ! "

" Can-dee ! "

You continue your wanderings and you strike a nigger district. Negresses and their beaux are flirting in corners

3 *a*

and on doorsteps. Darky boys and girls are skirling in
the roadway. Smartly dressed young men, carrying canes,
come giggling and pushing one another on the pavement,
crying out music-hall catches—" Who was you with last
night ? " and the like.

You know the habitat of the Jew by the abundance
of junk-shops, old-clothes shops, and offices of counsellors-
at-law. It seems the Jews are very litigious, and even
the poorest families go to law for their rights. You find
windows full of boxing-gloves, for the Jews are great boxers
in America. You find stalls and push-carts without end.
And every now and then rubbish comes sailing down from
a window up above. That is one of the surest signs of
the Jews being installed—the pitching of cabbage-leaves and
fish-bones and sausage-parings from upper windows.

What a sight was Delancey Street, with its five lines
of naphtha-lit stalls, its array of tubs of fish and heaps of
cranberries, its pavements slippery with scales, the air
heavy with the odour of fish !

On one of the first of my nights out in the New York
streets I came on a most wonderful sight. After prolonging
a journey that started in the centre of the city I found
myself suddenly plunging downward among dark and
wretched streets. I was following out my zigzag plan,
and came at last to a cul-de-sac. This was at the end of
East Ninth Street. It was very dark and forbidding ;
there were no shops, only warehouses and yards. There
were no people. I expected to find a new turning to the
left, and was rather fearsome of taking it even should I
find it. But at length I saw I had come to the East River.
At the end of the street the water lapped against a wooden
landing-stage, and there I saw a picture of wonder and
mystery.

High over the glimmering water stood Brooklyn Bridge,

with its long array of blazing electric torches and its procession of scores of little car-lights trickling past. The bridge hung from the high heaven by dark shadows. It was the brightest ornament of the night. I sat on an overturned barrow and looked out. Up to me and past me came stalking majestic ferry-boats, all lights and white or shadowy faces. Far away on the river lay anchored boats with red and green lights, and beyond all were the black silhouettes of the building and shipping on Long Island Shore.

. . . . . .

It was interesting to me to participate in the Russian Easter in New York, having lived in the Protestant and Roman Catholic Easters a whole month before on the emigrant ship on the day we reached New York. I came to the diminutive Russian cathedral in East Ninety-Fifth Street on Easter Eve at midnight. I had been at a fancy-dress party in the evening, and as fortune would have it, had gone in Russian attire ; that is, in a blue blouse like a Moscow workman. What was my astonishment to find myself the only person so dressed in the great throng of Russians surging in and out of the cathedral and the side street where the overflow of them talked and chattered. They were all in bowler hats, and wore collars and ties and American coats and waistcoats. They even looked askance at me for coming in a blouse ; they thought I might be a Jew or a German, or a foolish spy trying to gain confidences.

I shall never forget the inside of the cathedral at one in the morning, the vociferous singing, the be-shawled peasant girls, the tear-stained faces. Priest after priest came forward and praised the Orthodox Church and the Russian people, and appealed to the worshippers to remember that all over the Russian world the same service was

being held, not only in the great cathedrals and monasteries, but in the village churches, in the far-away forest
settlements, at the shrines in lonely Arctic islands, in the
Siberian wildernesses, on the Urals, in the fastnesses of the
Caucasus, on the Asian deserts, in Jerusalem itself. It
was pathetic to hear the priests exhort these young men
and women to remain Russians—they were all young, and
they all or nearly all looked to America as their new home.
On all ordinary occasions they longed to be Americans and
to be called Americans ; but this night a flood of feeling
engulfed them, and in the New York night they set sail
and looked hungrily to the East whence they came. They
held tapers. They had tenderly brought their cakes, their
chickens and joints of pork, to be sprinkled with holy water
and blessed by the priest for their Easter *breakfast*. It
was sad to surmise how few had really fasted through Lent,
and yet to see how they clung to departing tradition.

Coming out of the cathedral we each received a verbose
revolutionary circular printed in the Russian tongue :
" Keep holy the First of May ! Hail to the war of the
Classes ! Hurrah for Socialism ! Workmen of all classes,
combine ! "—and so on. In Russia a person distributing
such circulars would be rushed off to gaol at once. In
New York it is different, and " influences " of all kinds
are in full blast. I looked over the shoulders of many
groups outside the cathedral on Easter Day, and found
them reading those New York rags, which are conceived
in ignorance and dedicated to anarchism. It seems the
Russian who comes to New York is at once grabbed by
the existent Social-Democratic organisations, and though he
go to church still, he begins to be more and more attached
to revolutionism. It is strange that these organisations are
directed, not against the Tsar and the officialdom of Russia,
but against the Government of the United States and the

commercial machine. There is no question of America being a refuge for the persecuted Russian. The latter is assured at once that America is a place of even worse tyranny than the land he has come from. But if he does not take other people's word he soon comes to that conclusion on his own account. For he finds himself and his brothers working like slaves and drinking themselves to death through sheer boredom, and he finds his sisters in the "sweat-shops" of the garment-workers, or loses them in houses of evil.

. . . . . .

I shall long remember the Night Court on Sixth Avenue, and several occasions when I entered there after midnight and found the same shrewd, tireless Irish judge nonchalantly fining and sentencing negresses and white girls found in the streets under suspicious circumstances. Many a poor Russian girl was brought forward, and called upon to defend herself against the allegations of the soulless spies and secret agents of the American Police. I listened to their sobs and cries, their protests of innocence, their promises of repentance, till I was ready to rise in Court and rave aloud and shriek, and be pounced upon by the great fat pompous usher who represses even the expression on your features. "Why," I wanted to cry aloud, "it is America that ought to be tried, and not these innocent victims of America—they are the evidence of America's guilt and not the committers of her crimes!" But I was fixed in silence, like the reporters doing their jobs in the front bench, and the unmoved, hard-faced attendants and police by whom the order of the Court was kept.

Then, not far along the same road in which the Night Court stands, I came one evening into a waxwork show of venereal disease. It was quite by chance I went in, for there was nothing outside to indicate what was within.

Only the spirit of adventure, which prompted me to go in and look round wherever I saw an open door, betrayed me to this chamber of horrors.   There I saw, in pink and white and red, the human body in the loathsome inflammation and corruption of the city's disease.   Chief of all I remember the queen of the establishment, a hypnotic-seeming corpse of wax, lying full-length in a shroud in a glass case.   Just enough of the linen was held aside to show or suggest the terrible cause of her disease.   The show was no more than doctor's advertisement, and it was open in the name of science, but it was an unforgettable vision of death at the heart of this great city pulsating with life.

.   .   .   .   .   .

Then the splendour of Broadway, the great White Way, " calling moths from leagues, from hundreds of leagues," as O. Henry wrote.   What a city of enchantment and wonder New York must seem to the traveller from some dreary Russian or Siberian town, if seen aright.   It is a thrilling spectacle.   Now that I have looked at it I say to myself, " Fancy any man having lived and died in this era without having seen it ! "   Five hundred years ago the island was dark and empty, with the serene stars shining over it ; but now the creatures of the earth have found it and built this city on it, lit by myriad lights.   Thousands of years hence it will be dark again belike, and empty, and un-inhabited, and once more the serene stars will shine over the island.

V.

THE AMERICAN ROAD.

OUT in the country was a different America. The maples were all red, the first blush of the dawn of summer. In the gardens the ficaria was shooting her yellow arrows, in the woods the American dog-wood tree was covered with white blossoms like thousands of little dolls' nightcaps. Down at Caldwell, New Jersey, I picked many violets and anemones—large blue fragrant violets. The bride's veil was in lovely wisps and armfuls of white. The unfolding oak turned all rose, like the peach tree in bloom. Each morning when I awakened and went out into the woods I found something new had happened overnight,—thus I discovered the sycamore in leaf, fringing and fanning, and then the veils which the naked birch trees were wearing. The birches began to look like maidens doing their hair. The fern fronds and azalea buds opened their hands. The chestnut tree lit up her many candles. The shaggy hickory, the tree giant whose bark hangs in rags and clots, had looked quite dead, but with the coming of May it was seen to be awaking tenderly. In the glades the little columbines put on their pink bonnets. Only the pines and cedars were dark and changeless, as if grown old in sin beside the tender innocence of the birches.

It is very pleasant living in the half-country—living, that is, in the outer suburbs of the great American city or in the ordinary suburbs of the small city. New York has very little corresponding to our Walthamstow, Enfield,

Catford, Ilford, Camberwell, and all those dreary congested parishes that lie eight to ten miles from the centre of London. The American suburbs are garden cities without being called so. Each house is detached from its neighbour, there is a stretch of greenest lawn in front of it, there is a verandah on which are fixed hammocks and porch-swings, there are flower-beds, blossoming shrubs, the shade of maples and cherry trees. There are no railings or fences, and the people on the verandah look down their lawn to the road and take stock of all the people passing to and fro.

Working men and women live a long way out, and are content to spend an hour or an hour and a half a day in trains and cars if only to be quite free of the city when work is over.

Twelve miles of garden city is very wearisome to the pedestrian ; but he tramps them gaily when he remembers that the country is ahead, and that he has not simply to retrace his footsteps to a town-dwelling which for the time being he calls home.

I set off for Chicago in the beginning of May—not in a Pullman car, but on my own feet ; for in order to understand America it is necessary to go to America, and the only way she can be graciously approached is humbly, on one's feet. I travelled just in the same way as I have done the last four years in Russia—viz. with a knapsack on my back, a staff in my hand, and a stout pair of boots on my feet. I carried my pot, I had matches, and I reckoned to buy my own provisions as I went along, and to cook what was necessary over my own fire by the side of the road. At night I proposed to sleep at farmhouses in cold weather, and under the stars when it was warm. I was ready in mind and body for whatever might happen to me. If the farmers proved to be inhospitable, and would not take me

in on cold or rainy nights, I would quite cheerfully tramp
on till I came to a hotel, or a barn, or a cave, or a bridge,
or any place where man, the wanderer, could reasonably
find shelter from the elements.

I took the road with great spirits. There is something
unusually invigorating in the American air. It is marvellously healthy and strength-giving, this virginal land.
Every tree and shrub seems to have a full grasp of life,
and outbreathes a robust joy. It is as if the earth itself
had greater supplies of unexhausted strength than Europe
has—as if, indeed, it were a newer world, and had spent
less of the primeval potencies and energies bequeathed to
this planet at her birth. How different from tranquil and
melancholy Russia !

America is more spacious in New York State than in
New York City. The landscape is so broad that could
Atlas have held it up, you feel he must have had fine arms.
Your eyes, but lately imprisoned so closely by unscalable
sky-scrapers, run wild in freedom to traverse the long
valleys and forested ridges, waking the imagination to
realise the country of the Indians. There is a vast sky
over you. The men and women on the road have time to
talk to you, and the farmer ambling along in his buggy is
interested to give you a lift and ask after your life and your
fortunes ; and when he puts you down, and you thank
him, he answers in an old-fashioned way :

" You're welcome ; hand on my heart."

In the city no one has a word to say to you, but in the
country every one is curious. It is more neighbourly to be
curious and to ask questions. I rejoiced in every scrap of
talk, even in such triviality as my chat with Otto Fried-
richs, a workman, who hailed me at East Berne.

" Are you an Amarikan ? "

" No."

" Sprechen Sie deutsch, mein Herr ? "

" No ; I'm English."

" That bag on your back is made in Germany."

" Very likely," said I ; " I bought it in London."

" You running avay in case dere should be ze war, eh ? "

" Well, it would be safer here, even for you."

" What you think of our Kaiser ? "

" Fine man," said I.

" Some say ze Kaiser is too English to make ze war. But do you know wat I read in ze newspaper ? Der Kaiser cut his hand by accident, zen he hold up his finger—so, viz ze blood on it, and he say, ' Dat is my las' blood of English tropp,' and he . . . the blood away."

Not knowing the word for " flicked " Otto told me in dumb show with his fingers.

" Last drop of English blood, eh ? " said I.

" Yes."

" So he's quite German now, and ready to fight."

As I sat at the side of the road every passer-by was interested in my fire and my pot. They pitied me when they saw me trudging along the road, and when I told them I was tramping to Chicago they commonly exclaimed :

" Gee ! I wouldn't do that for ten thousand dollars."

But when they saw me cooking my meals they stopped and looked at me wistfully—that was their weakness; a hankering, not after the wilderness, but for the manna there. They addressed to me such non-pertinent remarks as :

" So that's how you fix it."

" I say, you'll get burned up."

" Are yer making yer coffee ? "

There was a great doubt as to my business, as the following interlocutions will suggest. In Russia I should be asked :

" Where are you going ? "

" To Kieff," I might answer.

" To pray," the Russian would conclude. But in America I was most commonly taken to be a pedlar.

" Whar you going ? "

" Chicago," I answered.

" Peddling ? "

It astonished me to be taken for a pedlar. But I was almost as commonly taken to be walking for a wager. I was walking under certain conditions. I must not take a lift. I must keep up thirty miles a day. I was walking to Chicago on a bet. Some one had betted some one else I wouldn't do it in a certain time. I took only a dollar in my pocket, and was supporting myself by my work. I lectured in school-houses, mended spades, would lend a hand in the hayfield. Or I was walking to advertise a certain sort of boot. Or I was walking on a certain sort of diet to advertise somebody's patent food. I was repairer of village telephones. I was hawking toothpicks, which I very cunningly made in my fire at the side of the road. I was a tramping juggler, and would give a show in the town next night.

Every one thought I accomplished a prodigious number of miles a day. At least a hundred times I was called upon to state what was my average " hike " for the day. Some were sympathetic and explained that they would like to do the same, to camp out ; it was the only way to see America. A girl in a baker's shop told me she had long wanted to tramp to Chicago and sleep out every night, but could get no friend to accompany her. Jews slapped me on the back and told me I was doing fine. Especially I remember a young man who walked by my side through the streets of Wilkes Barre. He told me his average per day had been forty-five miles.

"How long did you keep that up?" I asked.

"A week, we went to Washington."

"That's going some," said I.

"How far do you usually go?" asked he.

"Oh, five or six miles when the weather's fine," said I.

"Yer kiddin us!"

I was told that I wasn't the only person on the road. The great Weston was behind me, patriarch of "hikers," aged seventy-five. He wore ice under his hat, and was walking from New York to St. Paul at twenty-five miles a day, and was accompanied by an automobile full of liquid food. Far ahead of me was a woman in high-heeled boots tramping from New York to San Francisco. She carried only a small handbag, walked with incredible rapidity, and was proving for a newspaper that it was just as easy to walk in Vienna boots as in any other. Several weeks before me a cripple had passed, wheeling a wheelbarrow full of picture-postcards of himself, which he sold at a nickel each, thereby supporting himself. He was going from Philadelphia to Los Angeles, but had five years to do it in.

For all and sundry upon the road I had a ready smile and a greeting; almost every one replied to me at least as heartily, and many were ready to talk at length. Some, however, to whom I gave greeting either took me for a disreputable tramp or felt themselves too important in the sight of the Lord. When I said, "How d'ye do?" or "Good morning" they simply stared at me as if I were a cow that had mooed. In my whole journey I encountered no hostility whatever. Only once or twice I would hear a woman in a car say truculently to her husband, "There goes Weary Willie."

I had pleasant encounters innumerable, and many a talk with children. I felt that as I was in search for the emerging American, the American of to-morrow and the day after, I ought to take the children I met rather seriously. It was surprising to me that the grown-ups upon the road said to me always, " How-do ? " but the children said, " Hullo." The children always spoke as if they had met me before, or as if they were dying for me to stop and talk to them and tell them all about the road, and who I was and what I was doing.

At a little place called Clarkville I had a breakfast party. Perhaps I had better begin at the beginning. It had been a hard frosty night, and I slept in a barn on two planks beside an old rusty reaping-machine. At five in the morning I made my first fire of the day, and I shared a pot of hot tea with a disreputable tramp, who had come to warm himself at the blaze. By seven o'clock I had walked into the next village, about five miles on, and I was ready for a second breakfast. My first had been for the purpose of getting warm ; now I was hungry for something to eat.

It was a beautiful morning ; on each side of the road were orchards in full bloom, the gnarled and angular apple trees were showing themselves lovely in myriad outbreaking of blossom, and there were thousands of dandelions in the rank green grass beneath them. The sides of the roadway and the banks of the village stream were deep in grass and clover, and every hollow of the world seemed brimming with sunshine. The sun had been radiant, and he stood over a shoulder of the Catskills and poured warmth on the whole Western world.

On the bank of the stream I spread out my things, emptying out of my pack pots, cups, provisions, books, paper, pen, and ink. I gathered wisps of last year's weeds, and on a convenient spot started my little fire. I had just put eggs in to boil when the first of my party arrived. This was little Charles van Wie and his friend. Charles was hired to come early to the school-house and light the fire, so that the school would be warm by the time the teacher and the other boys and girls arrived. I did not know that I had pitched my camp just between the village and the school, on the way all the children would have to come. In America the school-house is always some distance from the village—this is so that mothers may not come running in and out every minute, and it is a good arrangement for other reasons. It gives every little boy and girl a walk, and the chance of having upon occasion extraordinary adventures.

Charles and his friend set to work to gather sticks for me, and saved me the trouble of rushing every now and then for fuel to keep up the fire. Then they hurried away to the school-house, but promised, excitedly, to come back as soon as they could.

Charles returned and asked me where I was going to, and what was my name and where I'd come from. I told him, and he took out a pocket-book and pencil and wrote all down.

Then other boys came and watched me make my coffee. The boys—they were all under twelve—had bunches of white lilac fixed in their coats. I sat and ate my food and chattered.

" Is the lilac for your teacher ? " I asked of a boy.

" I guess *not*," he replied.

There was a look of disgust on his face.

" Is your teacher strict ? "

" Some."

The boys all sat or sprawled on the grass and chaffed one another.

One of them was wearing a badge in his buttonhole, a white enamelled button, on which was printed very distinctly :

Every
D A M
Booster.

But the DAM, when you looked at it closely, turned out to be " Dayton's Adding Machines."

" What does ' booster ' mean ? " I asked.

" A feller that makes a job go," it was explained to me.

After breakfast I took a photograph of them sitting in the grass. They were much pleased.

" If Skinny Atlas had been here he'd have broke the camera," said one of them.

An extremely fat boy came into view and approached our party. The others all cried at him " Skinny Atlas," so I asked :

" Is that a nickname ?   Is his surname Atlas ? "

" No," they replied, " his surname is Higgins. But he's so darned fat that we call him Skinny Atlas. We have a saying, 'Put a nickel in the slot and up comes Skinny Atlas.' "

Accordingly all the boys cried out, " Put a nickel in the slot and up comes Skinny Atlas."

The fat boy, wearing a big straw sun-bonnet, came up and walloped several little boys. There was some horse-play round the embers of my fire, but Charles van Wie set an example by giving warning—

" Next person who pushes me I baste."

But it was getting late, and three little girls who had been hovering shyly at a distance cried out that it was time for the boys to go in.

The school had only fifteen pupils, boys and girls together, and they were all in one class, and they learned " the three R's," physiology, and the geography of the county they lived in.

The making of an American citizen is a simple matter in the country. And little Charles van Wie would make one of the best that are turned out, I should think.

Later on in the morning I went along to the school-house and peeped in at the window. There they all were, under the stern sway of a little school-mistress. But they didn't see me.

How useful to the tramp is the custom of hanging in the school-room a map of the county or of the state in which the children live. Often when I have wanted to know where I was I have clambered to the school-house window and consulted the map on the wall.

Once more to the road. The American highroad differs considerably from any way in Europe. Every farm-house has a white letter-box on a post outside its main entrance, and the farmer posts his letter and hoists a metal flag as a signal to the peripatetic postman that there are letters to collect. There are no thatched cottages; the home-steads stand back from the road, they are always of wood, and have shady verandahs and cosily furnished front rooms. The fields on each side of the road are protected by six-inch mesh steel netting, turned out by some great factory in Pittsburg I suppose. There are very few country guide-posts, and in New York State those there are come rather as a reward to you after you have guessed right. They are put up at a distance from the cross-roads. The pointers of the guide-posts are of tin. The telephone cones are of green glass, the poles are mostly chestnut, are not straight, and rot quickly. There are many advertisements by the way, and as you approach a town of importance they are as thick as fungi. They are not written for tramps to jeer at, but as hints to rich motorists. Still one necessarily smiles at :

CLOTHE YOUR WHOLE FAMILY ON CREDIT
$1 A WEEK

OR

DUTCHESS TROUSERS. TEN CENTS A BUTTON.
A DOLLAR A RIP.

A great portion of the State of Indiana seems to be devoted to Dutchess trousers, and I often wonder whether the company had to pay many indemnities to customers.

One sorry feature of country advertising was the number of notices scrawled in black with charcoal or painted in tar. In Europe picnickers write their names or the names of their sweethearts on the rocks and the walls and palings, but in America they write their trade, the thing they sell, and the price a pound, what O. Henry would call their especial sort of " graft."

Then " rrrrrrr ! rhrhrh—whaup—ssh ! " the automobile appears on the horizon, passes you, and is gone. I have no prejudice against automobilists ; they were very hospitable to me, and carried me many miles. If I had accepted all the lifts offered me I should have been in Chicago in a week, instead of taking two months on the journey. But the farmers curse them. On one Sunday late in June I counted everything that passed me. The farmer commonly tells you that hundreds of automobiles whirl past his door every day. This day there were just one hundred and ten, of which thirty-two were auto-cycles and the rest cars. As a set-off against this there were only five buggies and three ordinary cyclists. That was one of the last days of June, when I was seventy miles from Chicago. I had two offers to take me into the city that day !

Besides counting the vehicles that passed me I took stock of the automobilists themselves. No one passed till 7 A.M., and then came a loving couple, looking like a runaway match. He was clasping her waist, and their trunks were roped on to the car behind. Then six young men, all in their wind-blown shirts, came tearing along on auto-cycles. Scarcely had the noise of these subsided when a smart picnic party rolled past in a smooth running car, flying purple flags, on which was printed the name of their home city—Michigan. This is a common custom in America, to carry a flag with the name of your city. It boosts your own town, and is thought to bring trade there.

Six townsmen came past me in a grand car. Their hats were all off ; they were all clean shaven and bald. Coats had been left at home, and the six were in radiantly clean coloured shirts. They smiled at me ; I was one of the sights of the road.

Many picnic parties passed me, and men and women called out to me facetiously. Six shop-girls on a joy ride came past, and one of them kissed her hand to me—that is one of the things the girl in the car can safely do when she is passing a pedestrian.

Family parties went by, and also placid husbands and wives having a spin before lunch, and bashful happy pairs sitting behind the back of the discreet chauffeurs. There came an auto-cycle with a frantic man in front and a girl astride on his carrier behind. She was wiping the sand out of her eyes as she passed, her skirt was blown by the wind, and she showed a pair of dainty legs ; the funny way in which she was obliged to sit made her look like a stalk bending over among reeds.

One of the few cyclists I met came up after this, and he dismounted to talk to me. He was a tender of gasoline engines " on vacation." I learned from him about the single auto-cycle for two. It appears that in America they manufacture special seats to screw on the back of a motor-bicycle ; some use that. Many, however, just strap a

cushion on. Young men who have auto-cycles have a
" pull " with the girls ; they pick them up and take them
to business, or take them home from business, and on holidays they take them for rides of joy. Several similar
couples passed me during the day.

All sorts of gear went by ; rich gentlemen in stately
pride, workmen with their week-day grime scarcely cleared
from their faces, gay girls with parasols, honeymoon pairs,
cars with men driving, cars with women at the wheel. The
automobile is far more of a general utility in the United
States than in England. Workmen, and, indeed, farmers
themselves—not those who curse—have their own cars.
They mortgage their property to get them, but they get
them all the same. Even women buy cars for themselves,
and are to be seen driving them themselves. In Great
Britain it is very rare that you see a woman travelling alone
in a car, but in America it is a frequent sight. Of course
in Russia, in the country, an automobile is still a rarity. I
passed last summer in a populous part of the Urals and did
not see a single car. I did not even see an ordinary bicycle.
The farther west you go the more you find the inventions
of the day taken advantage of. It is an important phenomenon in America ; it shows that there is a readiness to
adopt and utilise any new thing right off, directly it is discovered.

This readiness, however, results in a lack of seriousness.
Inexpert driving is no crime ; accidents are nothing to
weep over ; badly constructed cars are driven along loose
springy roads with blood-curdling speed and recklessness.
The pedestrian is vexed to see a car come towards him,
leaping, bounding, dodging, dribbling, like some tricky
centre-forward in a game of football. The nervous pedestrian has to climb trees or walls upon occasion to be sure
he won't be killed. And then the cars themselves go fre-

quently into ditches, or overturn and take fire. The car has become a toy, but it's dangerous for the children to play with.

Then the dust! Carlyle said there was nothing but Justice in this world, and he used the law of gravity as his metaphor, but he didn't consider the wind—alas, that the dust does not fly in front of the car and get into the motorist's eyes, but only drifts away over the poor tramp who never did him any harm.

The only horse vehicle I remarked on the road was the buggy, a gig with disproportionately large wheels, the direct descendant of the home-made cart. The buggy is still popular.

" Where've you been ? " asks one American of another.

" Oh, just buggying around," he replies.

But the buggy is staid and conventional. It belongs to the old censorious religious America. It is supremely the vehicle of the consciously virtuous. It is also a specially rural vehicle. I think those who ride in buggies despise motorists from the bottom of their hearts ; they think them vulgar townspeople, and consider motoring a form of trespass. But the automobilists are not prevented, and they bear no rancour. They haven't time to consider the countryman. The man in the buggy belongs to the past. In the future there will not be time to be condemnatory, and the man who stands still to feel self-virtuous will go to the wall.

The people who will continue to feel superior to the motorists will be tramps sitting on palings, grinning at them as they pass by. They also will remain the only people the motorists, rushing abreast of Time, will ever envy. However much progress progresses there will always remain those who sit on the palings and grin.

VI.

THE REFLECTION OF THE MACHINE.

AS I tramped from village to village I was surprised to see so much stained glass in the churches of the Methodists, the Congregationalists, and other Puritans. Until quite modern times stained glass belonged exclusively to the ritualistic denominations. The Puritan, believing in simplicity of service, and in spirit rather than in form, put stained glass in the same category as the burning of incense, singing in a minor key, and praying in Latin. It partook of the glamour of idolatry; it had a sensuous appeal; it blurred the pure light of understanding. The true Puritan meeting-place is one of clear glass windows, hard seats, and a big Bible. It seems a pity that a very clear profession of faith should be blurred by picture windows—and, let me add by way of parenthesis, cushioned seats and revivalist preachers.

I examined in detail the coloured glass of a fine " Reform Church " that I passed on the road. The windows were rather impressive. They were not representations of scenes in Holy Writ, they contained no pictures of saints or angels, of the Saviour, or of the Virgin. So they escaped the imputation of idolatry. They were just pictures of symbolical objects or of significant letters. Thus, one window was the bird and symbolised Freedom, another was an anchor and symbolised Hope, another was a crown and symbolised Eternal Life. In one window the letters C.E. were illuminated—meaning Christian Endeavour, I pre-

sume ; on another window was the open Bible, symbolising
the foundation of belief.   In every case the whole window
was stained, and the little symbolical picture was set against
a brilliant background.

It was all in good taste, and was a pleasant ornament,
which made the church look very attractive exteriorly.
But it was a compromise with a spirit not its own.   My
explanation is, some one must have wanted chapels to put
in stained glass.   Some one now has a great interest in making them put in stained glass.   He is the manufacturer
of that commodity.   He has put stained glass on the market
in such a way that every church is bound to have it.   And
he has devised a way of not offending the rigorous Puritans.
" What is wrong in coloured light ? " said he.   " Nothing.
It is only what you use it for.   We can use it to show the
things in which we believe."   If incense could be manu-
factured in such a way as to make millions of dollars it
would find its way somehow into the chapels.   I was walking one day with an itinerant preacher, a man who called
himself " a creed smasher."   He wanted to weld all creeds
into one and unify the Church of Christ.   " Think of commerce," said he, " already it has stopped the wars of the
nations ; in time it will calm the wars of the sects.   If only
the churches were corporations, and Methodists could hold
shares in Roman Catholicism, and Roman Catholics in
Methodism ! "

Commerce is exerting an influence that cannot be with-
stood.   To take another instance, it has provided America
with rocking-chairs and porch-swings.   Although the Americans are an extremely active people, much more so than the
British, yet their houses are all full of rocking-chairs, and
on their verandahs they have porch-swings and hammocks.
The British have straight-backs.

The Americans did not all cry out with one voice for

rocking-chairs and swings. The Pilgrim Fathers did not bring them over. The reason they have them lies in the fact that some manufacturer started making them for the few. Then ambition took possession of him and he said, " There's something in rocking-chairs. I'm going to turn them out on a large scale."

" But there aren't the customers to buy them," some one objected.

" Never mind, we'll make the customers. We'll put them to the people in such a way that they gotta buy. We'll make 'em feel there's going to be such an opportunity for buyin' 'em as never was and never will be again."

" You believe you'll succeed ? "

" We'll make it so universal that if a man goes into a house and doesn't see a rocking-chair and a porch-swing he'll think, ' My Lord, they've had the brokers in ! ' "

So rocking-chairs and porch-swings came. So, many things have come to humanity—many worse things.

I had just written this note, for I have written most of my book by the road, when I heard the following interesting talk about the town of Benton, Pennsylvania. I was walking from Wilkes Barre to Williamsport, and Benton is on the way. It is a place that has had many fires lately.

" Ah reckon ah know wot cleared Benton out more'n fires."

" What's that ? "

" Wy, otomobeeles ; mortgaging their farms to get 'em. There's not much in Benton. You couldn't raise a hundred dollars. It's the agents and the boosters of the companies that are mos' to blame, no doubt, but they're fools all the same who buy otomobeeles when they cahn pay their bills at the stores."

" What agents ? " I asked. " D'you mean commercial travellers ? "

" No. The agents in the town. Every little town has a man, sometimes two or three men, who are agents for the companies who manufacture the cars ; they are just like the insurance agents, and are always talking about their business, comparing makes of car, praising this one and that, and getting folks on to want them."

" I suppose the companies want to make the motor car a domestic necessity, a thing no one can do without," I remarked.

" You're right ; they do and they will. They'll fix that in time, you betcher, we'll all be having them. Then when we cahn do without 'em they'll raise the prices on us. Already they've started it with the gasoline ; there's plenty motor spirit in the world, but the company gets possession of it and regulates the prices. An' you cahn make an oto go without gasoline. They can put it on us every time."

I should say society at Benton was suffering very badly from the influence of depraved commercialism. Some years ago Miss Ida Tarbell exposed what has been called " The Arson Trust," a company formed for setting fire to insured establishments on a basis of 10 per cent. profit on the spoil. Benton might have furnished her with some interesting examples. There have been so many fires in the little town of late that tramps are refused the shelter even of barns, as if their match-ends were responsible. On the Fourth of July three years ago half the town was burnt down. Last year in a gale the shirt factory was gutted ; the workmen had banked the fire up for the night, and about twenty minutes after the last man had left the works there was an explosion, and the red coals were scattered over the wooden building. Two months ago a large house took fire, and just a week before I reached the settlement the large Presbyterian church was consumed. Indeed, as I came into the town I remarked with some surprise the charred

walls and beams of the church, and read the pathetic printing on the stone of foundation, " This stone was laid
in 1903."

I had an interesting account of the church from the wife
of a farmer at whose house I stayed a night.   The church
had been insured for seventeen thousand dollars, and it
was twelve thousand dollars in debt.   The money borrowed
was not secured on the church building, but on the personal
estates of many people in the town.   Consequently, several
people were liable to be sold up if the money were not forthcoming.   Two days before settling day the fire took place,
and there was doubtless rejoicing in some hearts.   The
villagers had tried hard to make the place pay, they had
even let a portion of the church building to be used as a
bank !   Bazaars had failed.   The debt-raiser had tried " to
put a revival over on to them," but had failed.   The min-
ister, not receiving his salary, had abandoned them, and at
last the bare fact remained of the big white church and the
big unpaid debt.   Then occurred the providential fire.

But the insurance company would not pay the seventeen thousand dollars.   The fire had taken place under
suspicious circumstances, and it was said there would be a
legal fight over it.   The conflagration had occurred on the
night of a school-opening meeting.   Choice flowers had
been sent from many houses in the town, and it was beautifully decorated.   There was, however, nothing obviously
inflammable in the church ; it was built largely of brick and
stone.   But about an hour after the people had gone home
the fire broke out.   Next day it was found that the big
Bible had been soaked in coal oil.   Oiled newspaper was
found, and it was alleged that the fire brigade would have
saved the church, but that as fast as they put it out in front
somebody else was lighting it up behind.   Anyhow, the
insurance company refused to pay the seventeen thousand

4

dollars. But it cannot refuse absolutely ; the advertisement of failure to pay would be too damaging—it will put up a new church instead ! The Presbyterian church will be resurrected.

" I put Benton up against the world for fires," said my hostess. " For a small place, only a thousand people, I reckon there isn't its like."

For my part I felt sorry for the Bentonians, even for those who set the fire alight, supposing it was deliberately lighted. When commercial interest is the greatest thing in the world there are opportunities for a few men to feel themselves great and powerful, but that glory of mankind is far overbalanced by the occasions on which it causes man to be mean. Commercial tricks bring the holy spirit of man into disrepute. To find oneself mixed up in certain machinations is poignantly humiliating. We have all of us been wounded in that way ere now. The just pride of the soul has been offended, and we have thought how shameful a thing it was to have become mixed up in it at all, by *it* meaning the world, the whole shady business, call it what you will.

As I went along from village to village in New York and Pennsylvania I was struck by the uniformity of the architecture. Every church and school and store and farmstead seemed standard size and " as supplied." There seemed to be a passion for having known units. Not only in architecture was this evident, but in every utensil, machine, carriage, dress of the people. It was evident in the people themselves. Americans have the name of being extremely conventional. I think that is because, under the present domination of the *commercial machine*, American boys and girls and men and women are all turned into standard sizes. If Americans have rigid principles of ethics it is because they believe all the parts of the great machine are standardised, and that when any one part wears out there must always be an accurately fitting other part ready to be fixed where the old one has fallen out. Personality itself is standardised ; thus the tailor-priest advertises his wear, " Preserve your Personality in Clothes. Occasionally you have observed some article of wear that has led you to the mental conclusion — ' That's my style — that's me.' "

It was strange to me to find that even tramps and outcasts, who fulfil little function in the machine, were expected to conform to type. I was stared at, questioned ; my rough tweeds, so suitable to me, were an object of mirth ; my action of washing my face and my teeth by the side of the road was a portentous aberration. I remember how astonished a motorist and his wife appeared when they came upon me in the act of drawing a pail of water for a thirsty calf one morning in Indiana. The temperature stood at ninety-five in the shade—all nature was parched, and as I came along the highway a calf, fastened by a chain to the steel netting of a field, came up and rubbed his nose on my knees. As calves don't usually take the initiative in this way, I concluded he expected me to do something for him. There was an empty pail beside him. I took it to the farmhouse pump and drew water. As I did so, the farmer and his wife drew up at the farm in their motor, and they looked at me curiously. The calf came bounding towards me and almost upset the pail in his eagerness to drink. Then he gulped down all the water, and whilst I went to draw another pailful he executed a sort of war-dance or joy-dance, throwing out his hind legs and bounding about in a way that testified his happiness. The farmer's wife broke silence :

" Wha' yer doing ? "

" I'm giving the calf some water."

" Nao," said she, and looked at her husband, " giving the calf some water, can—you—beat—that ? "

I gave the calf his second bucketful and then started off down the way again, and the farmer and his wife looked after me in blank surprise. In America no tramp has any compassion for thirsty calves, he is not expected to look after the thirst of any one but himself. The farmer and his wife looked at one another, and their eyes seemed to say, " But tramps don't do these things ! "

Thence it may be surmised that America is no place for individuals as such. Originality is a sin. Americans hate to give an individual special attention, special notice. Even personal salvation is merged in mass salvation. The revivalist, his press agents, and stewards are a means of wholesale salvation. A revival meeting is a machine for saving souls on a large scale. It might be thought that the revivalist himself took his stand as an exceptional individual. Not at all : he is only a type. American public opinion does not allow a man to stand out as superior. It is surprising the dearth of noble men in the popular estimate of to-day. Mockery follows on the heels of noble action or individual action, and reduces it to type. That is a great function of the American Press of to-day, the defaming of men of originality and the explaining away of noble action. I remember a conversation I heard at Cleveland. Roosevelt had just cleared himself of the press libel of drunkenness.

" Wasn't it a good thing to clear the air, so," said one man, " and get clear of the charge once for all ? "

" I don't think he got clear of it," said the other. " It's all very well to bring an action against the editor of a provincial paper, but why didn't he take up the cudgels against one of the powerful New York journals, who said the same thing ? They had money and could have defended their case."

"I don't think money was needed—except to buy evidence."

"If you ask me," said the other, "it was all a very shrewd electioneering dodge. Roosevelt is an expert politician. He knows the value of being in the limelight, and he knows that nothing will fetch more votes in the United States just now than a reputation for sobriety. He was just boosting himself and the home products."

That is a fair example of the way people think of striking personalities and original views.

Then every man is considered a booster. Boosting is accepted as a national and individual function. Towns are placarded: "Boost for your own city and its own industries. Make a habit of it." In Oil City, for instance, I found in every shop a ticket announcing "Booster Week June 9–16." In that week Oil City was going to do all it could to call attention to itself. Citizens would pledge themselves to speak of Oil City to strangers in the train and when on visits to other towns. The city of Newark, New Jersey, is always recommending its own people and visitors to "Think of Newark." Whenever you enter into conversation with an American you find him suddenly drifting towards telling you the name of a hotel to stay at, or of an establishment where they sell "dandy cream," or he is praising the bricks turned out by the local brick works, or the conditions of the employment of labour in some silk works on which his native town is dependent for prosperity. In a widely distributed "Creed of the American" I read, "I remember always that I am a booster." Even fathers refer to their new-born babies as "little boosters." It should be remembered when Americans are boasting of their native land and its institutions that they were cradled in boosting. It is a habit that in many ways has profited America. It has attracted the emigrant more than all that has ever been printed about it. It is a great commercial habit. But it is in the end degrading.

What is the name of the fairy who has muttered an incantation over the Pilgrim Father and changed him into a booster ? And is a booster only a Pilgrim Father who brags about the stuff he manufactures ?

It seemed to me that by substituting the idea *booster* for the idea *man* you get rid of so many of the weaknesses of flesh and blood. A man who is boosting day in and day out, using his tongue as a sort of living stores' catalogue, is necessarily loyal to the great machine. But loyalty to the machine has its dangers. On my journey to Chicago I made some interesting observations in Natural History. I got into the train at Franklin to go to Oil City, some five or six urban miles. What was my astonishment to see that each of the eight or nine passengers in my car had fixed their railway tickets in the ribbons of their hats, and they themselves were deep in their newspapers. The conductor came along and took the tickets from their hats and examined them, collected those that were due to be given up and punched those that were not, and stuck them back in the ribbons of the hats, the wearers reading their newspapers all the time and making not the slightest sign that they noticed what the conductor was doing. The only sign of consciousness I observed was a sort of subtle pleasure in acting so—the sort of mild pleasure which suffuses the faces of lunatics when they are humoured by visitors to the asylum. They were shamming that they were machinery, and in almost the same style as the man who is under the delusion that he is a teapot, one arm being his spout and the other his handle.

Thus the elevator man in the Department Store also thinks himself a bit of machinery. He seems to be trained to act mechanically, and never to alter the staccato patter that comes from his mouth at each floor. He speaks like a human phonograph.

Then all waiters, shop-attendants, barbers, and the like try to behave like manikins. Most of all, in the language of Americans is the mechanical obsession apparent. A man who is confined in a hospital writes : " I'm *holding down a bed* in the hospital over here." The man who meets another and brings him along, simply " collects " him in America. The baseball team that beats another 6–0 " slips a six-nothing defeat " on them. Especially in baseball reports, commercialism and rhythms heard in great " works " abound.

The influence of great machinery gets to the heart of the people. A man when he joins a gang of workmen is taught to co-operate ; he has to trim off any original or personal way of doing things, and fit in with the rest of the gang. When the gang is going mechanically and easily, a man quicker than the rest is taken as leader, and the speed of the work is raised. The mechanical action in each individual is intensified, is perfected. Cinematograph films are even taken of gangs at work ; the pictures are shown before experts, who indicate weak points, recommend discharges or alterations and show how the gangs can be reconstituted to work more smoothly. Each man is drilled to act like a machine, and the drilling enters into the fibre of his being to such an extent that when work is over his muscles move habitually in certain directions, and the rhythm of his day's labour controls his language and his thought.

In the factory it is the same. In a vast mechanical contrivance there is just one thing that machinery cannot do ; so between two immense complicated engines it is necessary to place a human link. A man goes there, and flesh and blood is grafted into steel and oil. The man performs his function all day, but he also senses the great machine in his mind and his soul ; and when he goes out to vote for his President, or talk to men and women about the world in which he lives, he does so more as a standardised bit of mechanism, than as a tender human being.

Alas for the men and women who wear out and cease to be serviceable ! They are the old iron, and their place is the scrap-heap. " White trash " is the name by which they go.

Bernard Shaw, and indeed many others, look forward to the diminution of toil by machinery. The minimising of toil is to them a great blessing. Because machinery lessens toil they are on the side of machinery. Meanwhile life shows a paradox. The Russian peasant who works without machines toils less than the American who takes advantage of every invention. The Russian emigrant who comes to America simply does not know what work is, and he stares in amazement at the angry foreman who tells him, when he is at it at his hardest, to " get a move on yer."

In America the Americans slave ; they slave for dollars, for more business, for advancement, but in the end for dollars only, I suppose. They will fill up any odd moment with some work that will bring in money. They will make others work, and take the last ounce of energy out of their employees. The machine itself is the size of America, and only in little nooks and corners can anything spring up that is not of the machine. Even millionaires know nothing more to do than to go on making millions. Yet there is not a feverish anxiety to get money. Losses are borne with equanimity. It's just a matter of " the apple tree's loaded with fruit. I'm going up to get another apple."

Present experience shows that machinery increases the toil of mankind. It need not increase it, but it does. It might diminish it, but there are many reasons why it does not. For one thing, it increases the standard of living. It makes rocking-chairs, porch-swings, automobiles, and the like indispensable things. First, machinery makes the things, then the things make the machinery duplicate themselves. So it raises the standard of living and increases the toil of mankind. It is going on increasing the standard of living for the rich, for the middle-class aping the rich, and for the working men aping the middle-class.

Is it good, then, that the standard of living is being raised? Well, no; because the standard of living now means the standard of luxury. I should have used that phrase from the beginning.

I said this to a man on the road, and he asked me what I thought a man should live for, but I could not answer him. Each man has his individual destiny to fulfil. Destiny is not a matter of the clothes you wear or of the cushions you sit upon. The beggar pilgrim going in rags to Jerusalem may be more happy than a Pierpont Morgan, who writes pathetically at the head of the bequest of his millions that he believes in the blood of Jesus.

One thing I noted in America, that the blossom of religion seems to have been pressed between Bible leaves, withered and dried long ago. What is called religion is a sort of ethical rampage. The descendants of the Puritans are " probing sin " and " whipping vice." The rich are signing cheques, the hospitals are receiving cheques. The women of the upper classes are visiting the poor and adopting the waifs. But seldom did I come in contact with a man or a woman who stood in humble relation to God or the mystery of life. Even the great passion to put things right, lift the masses, stop corruption, and build beautiful cities and states is begotten in the sureness of science rather than in the fear of the Lord. Far from fearing God, preachers announce from their pulpits that they are " work-

4 a

ing with Him," or " co-operating with the inevitable tendencies of the world," or " hastening on the work of evolution."
For my part I believe that it is my sacred due to my brother
that he be given an opportunity of facing this world, the
mystery of its beauty and of his life upon it, that he find
out God for himself and learn to pray to Him. But that
is at once Eastern and personal.

The Y.M.C.A. informs me as I sit in a car that " The
great asset of this town is the young men of this town."
Must it be put that way ? Is that the only way in which
the people of the town can be got to understand how wonderful is the life and promise of any young man, how tender
and gentle and lovable he is personally, how unformed, how
fresh from his mother and his Creator ?

As I go along the road I pick up tracts, sown by the
devil, I suppose. Here is one of them :

Verily I say unto you that each and every one of you
may be a Count of Monte Christo, and some day exclaim,
" The World is mine ! "

The world was made for you, that I know. That you
were made for the world goes without saying.

Therefore hear me and believe me. If you desire wealth
it *can* be yours. If you desire *fame* it can be yours.

But you cannot get something for nothing. You must
pay for everything worth having. You must pay the price
set upon it, and in the coin of the realm.

The coin of the realm is industry—just that. Industry
and only industry. Nothing but industry.

Poor immigrant, who thinks it would be grand to be a
Count of Monte Christo, or, to bring it nearer home, a
John D. Rockefeller or an Andrew Carnegie, and who
thinks that honest labour will take him there ! Even were
American success a thing worth striving for it is not won
by that means. It is a game of halma. It's not the man

who moves all his pieces out one square at a time who wins, but the sagacious player who knows both to plan a advance and to hop over others when the opportunity rises.

But the good American young man, " the greatest asset f the town," believes this gospel, and he gives his body and mind to the great machine, and fills the gap between two otherwise disconnected mechanisms. If he has been brought up " well," he justs fits the gap and is standard size. He feels in his soul every throb of the engines, and registers in his integuments every rhythm and rhyme of the great, accurate, definite, circulating, oscillating machine. He behaves like a machine in his leisure hours. He even dances like a mechanical contrivance. On none of the occasions when the Fatherland requires his sober human judgment can he stand as a man. He seems spoilt for the true citizenship. What he does understand is the improvement, adjustment, and significance of machinery, and he can look intelligently at America the Great Machine. Perhaps this is his function whilst America is realising the dream of materialism and progress. But America would take care of itself if the American were all right. I could not but have that opinion as I left the cities and walked through the rich country, the new world, as yet scarcely visibly shop-soiled by commercialism.

VII.

RUSSIANS AND SLAVS AT SCRANTON.

I CAME into Forest City along a road made of coal-dust. A black by-path led off to the right down a long gradual slope, and was lost among the culm-heaps of a devastated country side. Miners with sooty faces and heavy coal-dusty moustaches came up in ones and twos and threes, wearing old peak-hats, from the centre of the front of which rose their black nine-inch lamps looking like cockades. They carried large tarnished "grub-cans," they wore old cotton blouses, and showed by unbuttoned buttons their packed, muscular bodies. Shuffling forward up the hill they looked like a different race of men—these divers of the earth. And they were nearly all Russians or Lithuanians or Slavs of one kind or another.

"Mostly foreigners here," said I to an American whom I overtook.

"You can go into that saloon among the crowd and not hear a word of white the whole night," he replied.

I addressed a collier in English.

"Are you an American?"

"No speak English," he replied, and frowned.

"From Russia?" I inquired, in his own tongue.

"And you from where?" he asked with a smile. "Are you looking for a job?"

But before I could answer he sped away to meet a trolly that was just whizzing along to a stopping-place.

Presently I myself got into a car and watched in rapid procession the suburbs of Carbondale and Scranton. Black-faced miners waited in knots at the stations all along the road. I read on many rocks and railings the scrawled advertisement, "Buy diamonds from Scurry." Girls crowded into the car from the emptying silk-mills, and they were in slashed skirts, some of them, and all in loud colours, and over-decorated with frills, ribbons, and shoddy jewellery. We came to dreary Iceville, all little grey houses in the shadow of an immense slack mountain. We came into the fumes of Carbondale, where the mines have been on fire ten years ; we got glimpses of the far, beautiful hills and the tender green of spring woods set against the soft darkness of abundant mountains. We dived into wretched purlieus where the frame-buildings seemed like flotsam that had drifted together into ridges on the bending earth. We saw dainty little wooden churches with green and yellow domes, the worshipping places of Orthodox Greeks, Hungarians, Ruthenians, and at every turn of the road saw the broad-faced, cavernous-eyed men and the bright-eyed, full-bosomed women of the Slavish nations. I realised that I had reached the barracks of a portion of America's great army of industrial mercenaries.

I stayed three days at Casey's Hotel in Scranton, and slept nights under a roof once more, after many under the stars. I suppose there was a journalist in the foyer of the hotel, for next morning, when I opened one of the local papers, I read the following impression of my arrival :

With an Alpine rucksack strapped to his back, his shoes thick with coal-dust, and a slouch hat pulled down on all sides to shut out the sun, a tall, raw-boned stranger walked up Lackawanna Avenue yesterday afternoon, walked into the rotunda of the Hotel Casey and actually obtained a room.

Every paper told that I was an Englishman specially interested in Russians and the America of the immigrant. So I needed no further introduction to the people of the town.

Just as I was going into the breakfast-room a bright boy came up to me and asked me in Russian if I were Stephen Graham. "My name is Kuzma," said he. " I am a Little Russian. I read you wanted to know about the Russians here, so I came along to see you."

"Come and have breakfast," said I.

We sat down at a table for two, and considered each a delicately printed sheet entitled, " Some suggestions for your breakfast." Kuzma was thrilled to sit in such a place ; he had never been inside the hotel before. It was pretty daring of him to come and seek me there. But Russians are like that, and America is a free country.

As we had our grape-fruit and our coffee and banana cream and various other " suggestions," Kuzma told me his story. He was a Little Russian, or rather a Red Russian or Ruthenian, and came from Galicia. Three years previously he had arrived in New York and found a job as dish-washer at a restaurant, after three months of that he progressed to being bottle-washer at a druggist's, then he became ice-carrier at a hotel. Then another friendly Ruthenian introduced him to a Polish estate agent, who was doing a large business in selling farms to Polish immigrants. As Kuzma knew half a dozen Slavonic dialects the Pole took him away from New York, and sat him in his office at Scranton, putting him into smart American attire, and making a citizen out of a " Kike." I should say for the benefit of English readers that illiterate Russians and Russian Jews are called Kikes, illiterate Italians are " Wops," Hungarians are " Hunkies." These are rather terms of contempt, and the immigrant is happy when he can speak and understand and answer in English, and so can take his stand as an American. After six months' clerking and interpreting Kuzma began to do a little business on his own account, and actually learned how to deal in real estate and sell to his brother Slavs at a profit.

Kuzma, as he sat before me at breakfast, was a bright, well-dressed business American. You'd never guess that but three years before he had entered the New World and taken a job as dish-washer. He had seized the opportunity.

" You're a rich man now ? " said I.

" So-so. Richer than I could ever be in Galicia. I'm learning English at the High School here, and when I pass my examination I shall begin to do well."

" You are studying ? "

" I do a composition every day, on any subject, sometimes I write a little story. I try to write my life for the teacher, but he says I am too ambitious."

" Do you love your Ruthenian brothers and sisters here ? "

" No ; I prefer the Great Russians."

" You're a very handsome young man. I expect you've got a young lady in your mind now. Is she an American, or one of your own people ? Does she live here, or did you leave her away over there, in Europe ? "

" I don't think of them. I shall, however, marry a Russian girl."

" Have you many friends here ? "

" Very many."

" You will take me to them ? "

" Oh yes, with pleasure."

" And where shall we go first ? It is Sunday morning. Shall we go to church ? "

We left the hotel and went to a large Baptist chapel.

When we arrived there we found the whole congregation engaged in Bible study. The people were divided into three sections,—Russians, Ruthenians, Poles. Russians sat together, Ruthenians and Little Russians together, and Poles together. I was most heartily welcomed, and took a place among the circle of Russians, Kuzma being admitted there also, though by rights he should have gone to the other Ruthenians. He was evidently a favourite.

We took the forty-second chapter of Genesis, reading aloud the first verse in Russian, the second in Ruthenian, and the third in Polish. When that was accomplished we prayed in Ruthenian, then we listened to an evangelical sermon in Russian, and then sang, " Nearer, my God, to Thee ! " in the same manner as we had read the chapter of Genesis—first verse in Russian, second in Ruthenian, third in Polish. It was strange to find myself singing with Kuzma :

> Do Ciebie Boze moj !
> Przyblizam sie.

I have never seen Poles and Ruthenians and Russians so happy together as in this chapel, and indeed in America generally. In Russia they more or less detest one another. They are certainly of different faiths, and they do not care about one another's language. But here there is a real Pan-Slavism. It will hold the Slavic peoples together a long time, and separate them from other Americans. Still there are not many cities in the United States resembling Scranton ethnologically. The wandering Slav when he moves to another city is generally obliged to go to a chapel where only English is spoken, and he strains his mind and his emotions to comprehend the American spirit.

After the hymn the congregation divided into classes, and talked about the Sermon on the Mount, and to me they were like very earnest children at a Sunday School.

I was able to look round. There were few women in the place ; nearly all of us were working men, miners whose wan faces peered out from the grime that showed the limit of their washing. At least half the men were suffering from blood-poisoning caused by coal bruises, and their foreheads and temples showed dents and discolorations. They had been " up against it." They would not have been marked that way in Russia, but I don't think they grudged anything to America. They had smiles on their lips and warmth in their eyes ; they were very much alive. " Tough fellows, these Russians," wrote Gorky. " Pound them to bits and they'll come up smiling."

They were nearly all peasants who had been Orthodox, but had been " converted " ; they were strictly abstinent ; they sighed for Russia, but they were proud to feel themselves part of the great Baptist community, and knit to America by religious ties. None of them entirely approved of Scranton. They felt that a mining town was worse than anything they had come from in Russia, but they were glad of the high wages they obtained, and were saving up either to go back to Russia and buy land or to buy land in America. They craved to settle on the land again.

It seemed to me Kuzma's business of agent for real estate among the Slavs was likely to prove a very profitable one. I shall come back to Scranton one day and find him a millionaire. He evidently had the business instinct—an example of the Slav who does not want the land again. The fact that he sought me out showed that he was on the *qui vive* in life.

When the service was concluded we went over the church with a young Russian who had fled to America to escape conscription, and who averred that he would never go back to his own country. His nose was broken, and of a peculiar blue hue, owing to blood-poisoning. His finger-nails were

cut short to the quick, but even so, the coal-dust was deep
between the flesh and the nail. He was most cordial, his
hand-shake was something to remember, even to rue a
little. He had been one of those who took the collection,
and he emptied the money on to a table—a clatter of cents
and nickels. He showed us with much edification the big
bath behind the pulpit where the converted miners upon
occasion walked the plank to the songs of fellow-worshippers.
They were no doubt attracted by the holiness of water,
considering the dirt in which they lived.

" He is a Socialist," said Kuzma, as we went away to
have lunch. " A Socialist and a Baptist as well. He has
a Socialist gathering in the afternoon and Russian tea and
speeches, and he wants me to go. But they hold there
should be no private property. I want private property.
I want to travel and to have books of my own, so I can't
call myself a Socialist."

In the afternoon Kuzma took me to the Public Library
and showed me its resources. In the evening we went to
supper at the house of a dear old Slovak lady, who had come
from Hungary on a visit thirty years ago, and had never
returned to her native land. She had been courted and
won and married within three weeks of her arrival—her
husband a rich Galician Slav. Now she was a widow, and
had three or four daughters, who were so American you'd
never suspect their foreign parentage.

She told me of the many Austrian and Hungarian Slavs
in Pennsylvania, and gave it as her opinion that whenever
a political party was badly worsted in South-eastern Europe
the beaten wanted to emigrate *en bloc* to the land of freedom.
When they came over they held to the national traditions
and discussed national happenings for a while, but they
gradually forgot, and seldom went back to the European
imbroglio.

A touching thing about this lady's house was a ruined chapel I found on the lawn—a broken-down wooden hut with a cross above it, built when the Slav tradition had been strong, and used then to pray in before the Ikon, but now only accommodating the spade and the rake and a garden-roller.

We had a long talk, partly in Russian, partly in English—the old lady had forgotten the one and only knew the other badly. So it was a strange conversation, but very informing and pleasant.

Slavs always talk of human, interesting things.

Kuzma was very happy, having spent a long day with an Englishman whose name had been in the newspaper. We walked back to the hotel, and for a memory he took away with him a newspaper cutting of a review of one of my books and a portrait of the tramp himself.

Next day, through the kindness of a young American whom I had met the week before entirely by chance, I was enabled to go down one of the coal-mines of Scranton, and see the place where the men work. The whole of the city is undermined, and during the daytime there are more men under Scranton than above it.

I was put into the charge of a very intelligent Welshman, who was a foreman, and we stepped into the cage and shot down the black shaft through a blizzard of coal-dust, crouching because the cage was so small, and holding on to a grimy steel bar to steady ourselves in the swift descent. In a few seconds we reached the foot—a place where there was ceaseless drip of water on glistening coal—and we walked out into the gloom.

Black men were moving about with flaming lamps at their heads, electric cars came whizzing out of the darkness, drawing trucks of coal. Whole trucks were elevated in the opposite shaft from that in which we had descended, elevated to the pit-mouth with a roar and a rush and a scattering of lumps of coal. I gained a lively realisation of one way in which it is possible to get a coal-bruise.

My guide showed me a map of the mine, and we went along dark tunnels to the telephone cavern, and were enabled to give greeting to miners as far as three miles away underground. Every man working in the mine was in telephonic communication with the pit-mouth. I saw the men at work, watched small trucks of coal being drawn by asses to the main line where the train was made up. I talked with Poles, Ruthenians, Russians—actually meeting underground several of those whom I had seen the day before in the Baptist Chapel. They were all very cheerful, and smiled as they worked with their picks. Some were miners, some labourers. The miner directs the blasting and drilling, puts in the powder and blows out the coal; the labourer works with pick and shovel. A man has to serve two years in a mine as a labourer before he can be a miner. Even a British immigrant, who has worked in South Wales or Northumberland or elsewhere, has to serve his term as a labourer. This discourages British men. Scranton used to be almost entirely Welsh; but it goes against the grain in an English-speaking man to fetch and carry for a Slovak or a Pole. On the other hand, this rule safeguards American strikers against imported miners.

After I had wandered about the mine a while I went up to the " Breaker's " tower, to the top of which each truck of coal was hoisted by the elevator; and I watched the fanning and screening and guiding and sifting of this wonderful machine, which in collaboration with the force of gravity can sort a ton of coal a second. I talked with Polish boys sitting in the stream of the rolling, hurrying coal; their task was to pick out bits of slate and ore; and I watched the platemen splitting lumps of coal with their long-handled hammers, and casting out the impurities. I saw the wee wash-house where the collier may bathe if he wish.

" Well, America or Russia, which is it ? " I asked of almost every Russian I met. " Which do you prefer ? Are you Americans now or Russians ? "

And nearly all replied, " America ; we will be Americans. What does one get in Russia ?—fifty cents a day." * Only a few said that America was bad, that the mining was dangerous and degrading. Strange to say, the astonishment at America's wealth and the wages they get from her had not died away. They admired America for the wages she gave ; not for the things for which the people of culture in the great cities admire her. America gave them money, the power to buy land, the power to buy low pleasures, the power to get back to Russia, or to journey onward to some other country—to the Argentine or to Canada.

I then spent a day visiting people at random. I went into Police Station No. 4, and found Sergeant Goerlitz sitting at a desk reading his morning paper, and he was very ready to talk to me. From him I gathered that the Slavs were the best citizens—quiet, industrious, and law-abiding. By Slavs he meant Huns, Bulgarians, Galicians, Ruthenians. The Russians were vulgar and pushing. He probably meant Russian Jews and Russians. The Italians were the most dangerous people ; they committed most crimes, and never gave one another away to the police. The Poles and Jews were the most successful people.

I went to the house of a communicative, broad-nosed, broad-lipped little Ruthenian priest—an Austrian subject—and he told me that Russia could take India whenever she wanted to, America could take Canada, and that Germany

* Fifty cents a day is very good pay for a miner in Russia ; thirty cents is quite a common wage.

would break our naval power. But the English would still be the greatest people in the world. In the near future the whole of North America would be one Empire, and the whole of South America another—one Anglo-Saxon, the other Latin. He was evidently a student of contemporary possibilities. Despite his belief in America he was proud of his own nationality, and jealous of the loss of any of his flock. To his church there came three hundred Little Russians and about thirty Great Russians. He reckoned there were fifty families in Scranton purely Nihilist—by that he meant atheistic and pleasure-seeking. At his church the service was in Slavonic and the sermon in Ruthenian. He was sorry to say there were comparatively few marriages. People came to the town to make money rather than to live.

Then I went to the official Russian priest, away on Division Street. He shepherded one hundred and thirty-seven families, and four hundred and sixty-two unmarried people. His church had been burned down the year before, but had sprung up again immediately. Some of the congregation had succeeded in business, and having come as poor colonists were now rich and respected citizens, professional men, large storekeepers, responsible clerks. Scranton was more like a Russian city than an American, and it was possible to flourish as a lawyer or a doctor or an estate agent although you knew very little of the English language. And out in the country round about were many Russian farms with real Russian peasants on them; and he spent many weeks in the year travelling about in the rural districts giving the consolation of Orthodoxy to the faithful.

A pathetic thing happened whilst I was taking leave of the priest; a young workman came in to ask advice, and in salutation he took the priest's hand to kiss it, but the latter was ashamed to receive that homage before me, and so tried to pull his hand away. Despite the churchman's enthusiastic account of his work I felt that little action was symbolical of the ebb-tide. It was to me as if I had looked at the sea of faith, and said, " The tide is just turning."

I visited the Y.M.C.A., so important an institution in America, giving a good room for fifty cents a day, and having its club-rooms, its swimming-baths, its classes for learning English. It wanted to raise seventeen thousand dollars in the forthcoming week, and many posters reminded passers-by that Scranton's greatest asset was not its coal or its factories or its shops, its buildings, its business, but its young men.

I walked the many streets at evening time when the wild crowd was surging in and out of the cinema houses and the saloons, and heard the American chaff and music-hall catch-words mixed with half a dozen Slavonic dialects. A young American engineer took me to several resorts, and initiated me in the mysteries of bull-dogs and fizzes, and as we went along the street he gave a running comment on the gaudily-attired girls of the town, whom he classified as " pick-ups," " chickens," and the like. At ten o'clock at night the streets were full of mirth, and all given over to sweethearting and flirting. Scranton's safety lies in the interest which the people have in one another, their sociability and general disposition to talk and hope. What it would be like if all these foreign mercenaries were mirthless and brutal it would be loathsome to picture. But I was surprised to find such lightness, such Southern frivolity in the people. It is strange that a people, most of whom are working all day in darkness, should take life so gaily. Even when they come up to the air of the outside world it is a bad air that is theirs, vitiated by the fumes of the burning mines; for at Scranton also the coal has been on fire ten years, and the smoke rolls from the slag-coloured wastes in volumes, and diffuses itself into the general atmosphere. One would think that the wretched framedwellings, ruined by the subsidence of the ground on which they were built, and begrimed with the smoke which factories belch all day, would disgust humanity. But it seems the man who works in dirt and ruin accepts dirt and disorder as something not wrong in themselves, quite tolerable, something even to be desired, a condition of freedom.

One day I met a young reporter, who was also a poet, and he took me to a point where there was a view of the city which he specially admired. It was a grey day—surely all days there are grey. We looked to the ridge of the West Mountain, a long dark wall built up to the sky, and many-roofed Scranton lay below it ; the thin spires of many conventicles pointed upward, and from numberless chimneys and spouts proceeded hardly moving white steams and smokes, all in strange curls and twists. Here and there were black chutes and shafts and mountains of slag, and the slates of the roofs of the houses glimmered appallingly under the wanness and darkening dusty grey of the sky.

" This sight does my heart good," said the poet. " It's good to live in a place like this where we're doing something."

" It would be a beautiful place if there were no Scranton here at all," I ventured.

" That's the glory of it," said he. " We have the faith to smash up the beauty of Nature in the hope of getting something better. It would be a beautiful world entirely if there were no such thing as man. Nature's beauty has no need of us. But we happen to be here. We have something in us that Nature could never think of. Scranton expresses man's passion more truly than the virginal beauty of the

Alleghany mountains or the valley of the young Susquehanna."

"A revolt against Eden," said I, "a fixed sullenness, man's determination to live in grime if he wants to—the children's infatuation for playing with the dirt."

"Oh, more than that," said the reporter poet. "Much more."

Perhaps.

That was perhaps a glimpse of the religion of America.

VIII.

AMERICAN HOSPITALITY.

IT is possible to distinguish two sorts of hospitality, one which is given to a person because of his introductions, and the other which is given to the person who has no introductions; the one given on the strength of a man's importance, the other on the strength of the common love of mankind. America is rich in the one species, she is not so rich in the other.

There is no country in the world where an introduction helps you more than in the United States. In this respect how vastly more hospitable the Americans are than the British! It is wonderful the extent to which an American will put himself to trouble in order to help a properly introduced visitor to see America. It is a real hospitality, and it springs from a great belief in America and in the American people, and a realisation of the fact that if nation and individuals are to co-operate to do things in the world, they must unbend and think of others beside themselves.

To me, in the literary and artistic clubs of New York, in the city institutions and schools, in the houses of the rich and cultured, and in the homes of the poor, America breathed kindness. New York seemed to me more friendly and hospitable than any other great city I had lived in. There also, as in Russia, one person came out and took me by the hand, and was America to me.

But when I shed respectability and the cheap fame of

having one's portrait and pages of "write-up" in the papers and put pack on back, and sallied forth merely as a man, I found that the other and more precious kind of hospitality was not easily come by. Little is given anonymously in the United States.

Not that the country people despise the tramp, or hate him or set the dogs on him, or even refuse him a breakfast now and then, but that they simply won't have him in their houses for the night, and are otherwise indifferent to his hardships. They do not look on the stranger as a fellow-man but as a loose wheel, a utility lying rusting in a field ; or at best they look upon him as a man who will " make good," who will get a job later on and *earn* his living. No one is good enough for the American till he has " made good." But this is the same in all commercialised countries, commercialism kills the old Christian charity, the hospitality of house and mind and heart.

In the old colonial days there was extraordinary hospitality in America, and this still survives in the West and North and South in places out of touch with the great industrial beehive of the East and Centre. The feeling still survives in the spirit that prevents Americans printing prohibitions. You never see the notice " Trespassers will be Prosecuted," though I do not know what one is to make of the uncharitable poster that frequently met my gaze in Indiana and Illinois :

KEEP OUT !

THAT MEANS YOU.

That is brutal.

Tramping up to Williamsport from Scranton I encountered forty-eight hours' rain, and only with difficulty on the second night did I obtain shelter. After being refused three times the first rainy evening, I found an old covered well beside an empty, padlocked shed. In this I spent twenty hours, sleeping the night and waking to a day of down-pour.

It was an interesting little hermitage ; the three walls were of stone, but the roof and floor of wood. One side of the building was completely open to wind and weather. In a corner was a dark square of clear water—the well. Half-way up the stone wall was a narrow ledge, and there I slept. I covered the ledge with two sacks ; for pillow I had a book, a duplicate pair of boots, and a silken scarf. I slept with my feet in a sack and a thick tweed coat spread over the rest of me,—slept well. By day I sat on a box and looked out at a deserted garden, and the rain pouring on the trees and rank grass. There were young pines and hemlocks and maples, and a shaggy hickory tree. Beyond them an apple orchard climbed over a very green hill, and the branches were all crooked and gnarled and pointing. The blossoms had shed their petals, and there was much young fruit.

I gathered dry wood and made a fire on the threshold, and dried wet wood and boiled a kettle, the smoke blowing in to me all the while, and the raindrops hissing and dying as they fell into the embers.

About midday a Dutch farmer came and stood in front of the little house, and stared for some minutes and said nought.

I hailed him : " Good day ! "

He did not reply to this, but inquired :

" Hev you not seen that notice on the wall—' Any one meddling with this house will be treated as he deserves ' ? "

I had not.

" Waal," said he, " it's there. So you'll put that fire out."

I complied.

" It's a wet day," said I.

" Yes, it's wet."

" I'd like to get put up for the night somewhere, and get a good meal. Do you know of any one who would do it ? "

He was silent for some while, and stared at me as if irritated, and then he said :

" Guess about no one in this hollow'd take any one in. But you might try at the store at the top of the hill."

" Couldn't you take me in ? "

" No ; couldn't do it."

" Then, could you put me up a meal ? "

" We have been out of food and are living on buckwheat cakes."

" I wouldn't mind some of them and some milk."

" No, no. No use. Wife wouldn't have any one in."

After some converse he learned that I was British, and he said, " There was one of yours here two-three years back."

" What did he think of this country ? "

" He said it was the darndest country he ever saw."

There was no help for it. I had to abandon the well and go out through the never-ceasing downpour and seek shelter and a decent meal. On my way to the store I met another farmer, and we had this interchange of talk :

" Can you put me up for the night ? "

" No."

" Can you make me up a meal ? "

" No."

" I'll pay you for it. You can have a quarter or so for a hot meal."

" We've just had our supper, and the women are doing other things now. There is a place on top of the hill."

A mile farther on I came to a General Store. It was

locked up, and as I stared into the window the owner eyed me from a house over the way.

He came out, looking at me apprehensively.

" Can you put me up for the night ? " I asked.

" No ; not to-night."

" Why not ? "

" We don't take only our own people. There's a place two miles on."

" Two miles through the wet."

" You're right."

" I can pay you what you get from your own people, and a little extra perhaps."

The storekeeper shook his head and answered :

" My wife is a little unwell and does not want the trouble."

" I can tell you you wouldn't get turned away like this in my country," said I.

" Where are you from ? "

" From England."

" Oh, wouldn't they ? "

" There are plenty of places where they'd take you in without charging for it. There are places in Europe where they'd come out and ask you into their houses on such a night."

" I dessay, I dessay."

" Well, I think the people about here are very inhospitable."

" I reckon you're right."

" I think you are inhospitable."

" Um ! "

" Well, you're a storekeeper ; I want some bread and some butter, and anything else you've got that doesn't need to be cooked."

" Are you hungry ? "

I told him I was, and he determined to be more charitable than I had given him the name for.

"Well," said he, "I can let you have a slice of bread
and butter and a cup of cawfee, I dessay."

"Thanks. I should like to buy a loaf of bread and a
quarter pound of butter, all the same," said I.

"We haven't any bread in the store. The baker leaves
it three times a week, and we've only enough for ourselves;
but I can let you have a slice, and that'll keep you going
till you get to Unityville. It's only about two miles away.
There's a hotel there. The folks have taken away the
keeper's licence, and you won't be able to get anything to
drink. But he'll take you in for a dollar. You'll get all
you want. In half an hour you'll be there. There are two
more big hills, and then you're there."

He brought the bread, and as I was ravenous I was
tamed thereby, and I thanked him. The bread and butter
and coffee were gratis. He was really a kindly man. I
shouldn't wonder if his wife had an acid temperament.
The night's lodging, no doubt, depended more on her than
on him.

I sat on rolls of wire-netting outside the store and
finished the little meal. Then I went away. Over the
hills in the dusk! It was real colonial weather; the light
of kerosene lamps streamed through the downpour of rain,
the dark woods on each side of the strange high road grew
more mysterious and lonesome, silent except for the throbbing of the rain on the leaves and on the ground. I stopped
at a house to ask the way, but when I knocked no one
answered. I looked through the kitchen window at the glow
of the fire and at the family round the well-spread table,
and the farmer's wife directed me through the glass."

At last—in a flow of liquid mud, as if arrested in floating
downhill—a miserable town and a hotel.

When I asked the host to put me up he said his wife had gone to bed with a headache, and if I had not rated him soundly I should have been turned into the rain once again.

"Well," said he, "I cahnt give you any hot supper, you'll have to take what's on hand."

So saying, he opened a tin of Boston beans, emptied them on to a plate, and put before me a saucerful of those little salt biscuits called oysterettes. My supper!

In the bar, deprived of ale, sat half a dozen youths eating chocolate and birch beer, and talking excitedly of a baseball match that was to be played on the morrow. Mine host was a portly American of the white-nigger type. The villagers, exercising their local option, had taken away his right to sell intoxicating liquor, and now on the wall he had an oleographic picture of an angel guiding a little girl over a foot-bridge, and saving her *from the water*. Somehow I think this was unintentional humour on the part of mine host. He was an obtuse fellow, who mixed the name Jesus Christ inextricably with his talk, and swore b'God. But he gave me a warm bed. And he had his dollar.

Another evening, about a month later, I sought a lodging in a town on Erie Shore. The weather was very hot, and I was tramping beside marshes over which clouds of mosquitoes were swarming. There was no good resting-place in the bosom of Nature, so I imagined in my heart, vainly, that I might find refuge with man.

I came to a town and went into the store and asked where I would be likely to find a night's lodging. The storekeeper mentioned a house in one of the by-streets. But when I applied there the landlady said her husband was away, and she would be afraid to have a stranger in his absence. I went to another house : they hadn't any room. I went to a third : they told me a man there was on the point of death and must not be disturbed. I returned to the store, and the storekeeper said it would be impossible to be put up for the night anywhere in the village. I told him I considered the harbouring of travellers a Christian duty.

" They don't feel it so about here," said he politely.

There was an empty park-seat at the end of the main street ; I went and sat on it and made my supper. Whilst I sat there several folk came and gazed at me, and thought I might be plotting revenge. In America they are very much afraid of the refused tramp—he may set houses on fire.

But I was quite cheerful and patient. I had been sleeping out regularly for weeks, and shelter refused did not stir a spirit of revenge in me. In any case, I was out to see America as she is, not simply to be entertained. I was having my little lesson—" and very cheap at the price."

But I found hospitality that night. As I sat on the park-seat a tall labourer with two water-pails came across some fields to me, passed me, and went to the town pump and drew water. " Surely," said I to myself, " that is a Russian."

I hailed him as he came back.

" *Zdrastvitye ! Roosky ?* "

I had guessed aright ; he replied in Russian.

" Are you working in a gang ? " I inquired.

" No, only on the section of the railway ; there are six of us. We have charge of this section. Where are you going to ? To Chicago ? Looking for a job ? Going to friends there ? Where are you going to sleep ? This village is not a good one. *Ne dobry.* If you sleep there, on the seat, up comes the politzman, and he locks you up. So you be three weeks late in getting to Chicago perhaps.

5

Why do you walk ? You get on freight train and you be there to-morrow or the day after. You come with me now. I sleep in a closed truck with five mates—four are Magyars, one is a Serb. It's very full up, and I don't know how the Magyars would take it if I brought you in. But I know a good place. A freight train is waiting here all night. There are plenty of places to sleep, and you go on in it to-morrow morning to Toledo."

He showed me an empty truck. I was very much touched, and I thanked him warmly.

" How do you believe," he asked in parting, " are you a Pole or are you Orthodox ? "

" Oh," said I, " I'm not Russian, I've only lived some years there. I'm a British subject."

This somewhat perplexed him. But he smiled. " Ah well," said he, " good-bye, *Sbogom*—be with God," and we parted.

A little later he returned and said that if I were lonely and didn't mind a crush, the Magyars would not object to my presence. But by that time I had swept the sawdusty floor of the truck, made a bed, and was nearly asleep. " Thanks, brother," said I, " but I'm quite comfortable now."

The Russians are a peculiarly hospitable people. Their attitude of mind is charitable, and even in commercial America they retain much of the spirit that distinguishes them in Europe. I met a queer old Russian tramp in Eastern Pennsylvania ; he exemplified what I mean. He was, however, rather an original.

In a district inhospitable to tramps I obtained my dinner by paying for it. In this way and by these words :

" Can you give me a meal for a quarter ? "

" Well, if you've got the coin I reckon we can do that."

I was sitting at a meal of canned beef, beans, and redcurrant jelly, sipping from a mug of coffee, in which might possibly be discerned the influence of a spoonful of milk. The farmer was cross-examining me on my business—where had I come from? Was I looking for a job? Was I walking for wager?—when a strange figure appeared at the window, a broad-faced, long-haired, long-bearded tramp in a tattered cloak.

He approached the house, and about ten feet from the window where we were sitting he stood stock-still, leaning on his staff and staring at us.

" A hobo—looks a bit fierce," said the farmer, opening the window. " How do? Wha—yer—want? "

" Give me a piece and a cup o' milk," said the foreigner.

" A Polander," said the farmer. " I guess I turn him over to the missus. Sue, here's a man wants a crust and some sour milk."

" Ee caant 'ave it," cried the farmer's wife.

" No go," said the farmer, and shook his head at the tramp.

The latter did not utter a word of reproach, but what was my astonishment to see him cross himself delicately, and whisper a benediction! A Russian, I surmised.

" It is not over-safe refusing them fellers," said the farmer. " They may burn your barn next night. I reckon Sue might have put him up something. Hear him curse as he went."

The old Russian was going eastward, I westward; but I resolved to turn back, carry him some bread, make some coffee, and exchange those tokens of the heart which are due from one wanderer to another upon the road. I hurried back and overtook him.

The old man was nothing loth to sit on a bank of grass whilst I bought a quart of milk at a farm. " Coffee, uncle," said I. " Russian coffee. Varshaffsky, such as you get at home in Russia, eh ? " Uncle smiled incredulously.

" Twigs, uncle, sticks, dry grasses ; we must make a fire," said I. Uncle got up and collected a heap of wood. My coffee-pot soon reposed on a cheerful blaze. The creamy milk soon began to effervesce and boil. In went six lumps of sugar and eight spoonfuls of coffee. Uncle recognised he was going to have a good drink when he saw that no water was to be added. It was a pleasure to see him with a mug of it in one hand and a hunch of good white bread in the other.

I learned that my friend was tramping his way to New York. At that city he would buy a ticket to Libau, and from Libau would walk home to his native village, or he would get under a seat in a train. He had come 250 miles of his journey from Minnesota in an empty truck of a freight train ; perhaps he would get another good lift before long.

" Why are you going home ? Can't you find work ? "

" Going to pray," said he. " I am going to my village to see my father's grave, and then to a monastery. I would finish my years in Russia and be buried in Russian ground."

" I suppose you didn't take root here ; American life doesn't suit you ? Didn't you like Americans ? "

" Well, I lived with other fellows from our village, and we succeeded sufficiently well. Some seasons we gained a lot of money. But I never felt quite at home. We reckoned we would build a church after a while—a high wooden one that one could see from the wheat-fields when we were at work. But my friend turned evangelical; he became a sort of molokan, and one by one all the other fellows joined him, and they went to meetings. I was the only one who remained orthodox. They reckoned I got drunk because I was orthodox; but I reckon I got drunk because they were evangelicals — because they had all deserted me, and I was lonely. It's hard on a man to be all alone."

"And why did you leave, uncle? What determined you to go?"

"I'll tell you. I had a strange dream. I saw my father, who is, as you know, dead long since and in his grave, and I saw a figure of St. Serge—St. Serge was his angel—and both lifted their arms and pointed to the East. I knew it was the East because there was a great red sunset behind them, and they pointed right away from it, in the other direction. When I wakened up I remembered this, and it made a great impression on me. I told Basil, my friend, who worked with me lumbering, and he laughed. 'But,' I said, 'that's not the thing to laugh at.' At last I decided to start for home. The idea that I might die in America and be buried there was always pricking me. I am not American. The American God won't take me when I die. Some of the fellows are going to take out their papers, because a Jew came round pestering them with books to learn English and prepare for examination, saying they ought to make themselves citizens; but that is not for me. I am Russian. Mother Russia! she is mine. They may keep you down and oppress you there, but the land is holy, and men are brothers.

"When I started home I was surprised that so many farmers said 'No,' when I wanted to sleep in their barns. I even got angry and shouted at them. But as I went further I got patient, and came to pray to God, every day and often, to give me my bread and bring me safely to Russia. Then I got peace, and never was afraid or angry, reckoning that even if I did die in America I should be dying on the way home, and my face would be turned towards Russia. I reckon that if I die my soul will get there just the same."

"It's not often that in Russia, when a man is refused bread, he says, 'Glory be to God!'" said I, recalling how the tramp had crossed himself after the farmer's refusal.

"No, not often. I thought out that for myself. At first I was silent when people turned me away. I gave thanks only when they took me in. But after a while my silence seemed a sort of impatience and angriness. So I recollected God even then, and crossed myself. A tramp has no ikons, so he needs all sorts of things to remind him."

The poor exile had told his story, and looked at me with dim, affectionate eyes. He held my hand tightly in his as we said "Good-bye"; he going eastward, I westward.

That was a way of living in the fear of God. That old man had real hospitality in his soul.

But in depicting the American farmer and storekeeper it would be unfair to characterise him as an inhospitable person. He is a great deal more hospitable than his actions would suggest. He is a kindly being. He has love towards his neighbour, and is more inclined to say "Yes" to the wanderer than "No." But he has often been victimised. He has been robbed, assaulted, insulted, his property has been damaged, barns set on fire, his crops in part destroyed by wilfully malicious vagabonds. The behaviour of the tramp is often a sort of petty anarchism; he has suffered in the heartless commercial machine, has got out of it only by luck, and his hand is against every man. He has cast over honour, principle, and conscience, and is able to gloat secretly over every little cynical act or meanness perpetrated at the expense of the good-natured but established farmer.

America has more tramps than any other country except Russia, and it would have more than Russia but for

the fact that there are often about a million pilgrim-tramps
on the Russian roads. The Russian tramp is, moreover,
a gentle creature; the American is often a foul-mouthed
hooligan.

In several little districts that I passed through I was
questioned by the farmers as to whether I belonged to a
gang of tramps who had been lurking in the neighbourhood
for weeks. A tramp was evidently regarded as an enemy
of society. Whenever I remarked on the inhospitality of
the people a rueful expression came over the farmer's face,
and he would begin to tell me that the old days were gone,
money was tighter, the cost of living was higher, taxes were
double, the land did not yield what it did of old, there were
many demands on them here; but out in the West it was
different. There, as in former times, every farm-house had
open doors and free table to the tramp and wanderer. No
one was more welcome than the tramp: he brought news
and stories of personal adventure; he might even be persuaded to do work in the fields.

I believe the Americans would be a truly charitable and
hospitable people if the evils of over-commercialism were
remedied, and if business were made kinder and more
human, and taxes were evenly distributed. There is an
immense good-will towards man in America: it is only
rendered abortive by mammon. I for my part have to
thank numberless farmers, east and west, for kindly interest
and good talks, loaves of bread, cups of coffee, and pleasant
meals. Several times when I have been cooking by the
side of a road a farm wife has come running out to me
with something hot from her kitchen, with an "Eat this,
poor man, and God bless you, you must be hungry."

Then the farmer's wife is often mollified when you are
able to buy her milk and eggs. She is the person who
counts in the farm. She must be approached; the husband

has very little say in what shall be given to the wanderer. As a fantastic old tramp said to me:

"Whilst you are yet afar off, the farmer's wife, standing on her threshold, espies you and takes you to be a hungry lion pawing the road and seeking whom you may devour. She calls to her husband, and he peereth at you. Perchance she fetcheth down the ancient blunderbuss from the wall; but when you come closer and hail her in English she says to herself with relief, even with pleasure, 'It is a man,' one of the attractive male species. You ask for bread and milk,—oh yes, she has it, and with a scared look still on her face, though transfigured with a mild gladness, she fetcheth you bread and milk and eggs; and then if you can pay her market price the scared look goes away entirely; and out of the goodness of her heart and the abundance of her pantry she addeth cookies and apple butter, and for these you pay nought—they are her favour. Don't ask her, however, to put you up for the night."

The tramp always has a hard time to get a night's lodging. A poor, weak, bedraggled Jew, whom I met shortly after the forty-eight hours' rain, told me that he had been all one night in the wet—his pedlar's pack had got ruined, he was suffering from pneumonia, and had thought that such weather meant sure death to him. He had tried every house in five towns and had been refused at every one. It was a sad comment on modern life.

In the Middle Ages, and in the days when Christianity meant more than it does now, the refusal of shelter was almost unheard of. And in peasant Russia to-day it would be considered a sin. An old pilgrim-tramp once said to me, "When we leave this world to get to Heaven we all have to go on tramp, and those find shelter there who sheltered wanderers here." But Americans will not be judged by that standard. The early Christians received strangers, and often entertained angels unawares; but the modern American is afraid that in taking in a strange tramp he may be sheltering an outcast spirit. Once tramps were angels; now they are rebel-angels.

IX.

OVER THE ALLEGHANIES.

BOTH the weather and the country improved before I reached Williamsport. On the height of the road to Hughesville I had a grand view of the mountains and of the sky above them, saw displayed green hills and forested mountains, and great stretches of ploughed upland all dotted over with white heaps of fertiliser. And the sky above was a battle-scene, the sun and his angels having given battle and the clouds taking ranks like an army. Glad was I to see to eastward whole battalions in retreat.

I passed through fine forested land with great hemlocks, maples, and hickories. A brawling stream poured along through the dark wood, and as I walked beside it a sudden gleam of sunshine pierced the gloom of foliage, and lit up boles and wet banks and wet rocks and the crystal freshets of the stream. Of all weathers I like best convalescent weather, the getting sunny after much rain. On the Sunday on which I reached the city the open road was swept by fresh winds, all the birds were singing, every blade of grass was conscious of rain taken in and of the sun bringing out.

Williamsport I found to be a peaceful, provincial town, well kept in itself and surrounded by beautiful scenery. It was looking its best in the freshness and radiance of a May morning. On its many hundred bright green lawns that run down so graciously from pleasant urban villas to

the roadway there was much white linen airing. Williamsport is an old lumbering town on a branch of the Susquehanna, and though that business has gone away, prosperity
and happiness seem to have remained behind. There was
a feeling of calmness that I had not experienced in other
American cities, and I felt it would be pleasant to live there
for a season.

I tramped down to Jersey Shore, and the night after
my halcyon day at Williamsport a thunderstorm overtook
me, shaking the old barn in which I slept and tearing away
rafters and doors. I witnessed Lockhaven under depress-
ing circumstances, but in any weather it must be an inferior
town to Williamsport, though it is also an old point for
lumbering on the Susquehanna.

The weather remained very rainy, and I was obliged
to forsake the atrociously clayey highroad for the cinder
track of the railway. In doing this I passed up into a
fine hilly country along the valley of the Beech Creek.
I came to Mapes (to rhyme with Shapes), but found it a
name and no more. A shooting and fishing resort with
one house in it. The Beech Creek was a fine sight, running along the base of the embankment of the railway,
carrying pine logs on its flood and racing the trains with
them, roaring and rushing, the logs pointing, racing, turning, rolling, toppling, colliding, but always going forward,
willy-nilly, getting clear of every obstacle and galloping
out of sight.

With one wet match I lighted a grand fire by the side
of the line, and boiled my kettle and dried myself and
chuckled. It might be going to rain more. I might be
going to have a queer night, but for the time being I was
having a splendid tea. It was a matter for consolation
in the future that on the wettest possible day it was not
difficult to light a fire with one match. The secret lies

in having plenty of dry paper in your wallet ; and I had
a copy of a New York Sunday paper, which lasted me to
light my fire all the way to Elkhart, Indiana, at least five
hundred miles' tramping.

The district of Mapes is one of the most beauteous in
the Alleghanies, or it was so this quiet evening. The
summits of the mountains were obscured by mists, but
up from the profound valleys the woods climbed, and the
lovely tops of trees seemed like so many stepping-stones
from the land up to cloudy heaven.

By the time I came to Monument it was dark. But
a great glowing brick-kiln looked out into the night, and
there were houses with many lighted windows. I was
directed to a workmen's boarding-house, and spent a night
among miners, railway men, and brick-workers. The
keeper of the establishment was doubtful whether he
would have me, but thought there was " one feller on the
third floor gone."

" What will be your charge ? " I asked.

" Well," said he, " a won't charge ye anything for the
bed, but the breakfast to-morrow morning will be twenty-
five cents."

" My ! " I thought, " here's something choice coming
along in the shape of a bed."

It turned out to be four in a room and two in a bed,
all sleeping in their clothes. There was even some doubt
as to whether there was not a fifth coming.

One man was in bed already ; I chose the unoccupied
bed, and laid myself upon it in full tramping attire. You
can imagine the state of sheets and quilts in a bed that
brick-makers and soft-coal miners sleep in in their clothes.

The man in bed was an Anglo-Saxon American. When
I said I was from England he asked me if I had walked
it all.

" I came by steamer of course to New York."

" How many days ? "

" Eight."

" Weren't you afraid ? " said he.   " Quite out of sight of land no doubt ? You wouldn't get me to go, not for many thousand dollars. That. *Titanic* was an affair, wasn't it. Fifteen hundred—straight to the bottom ! I'd have shot myself had I been there."

" What do you work at here ? "

" Brick-making."

" Lot of men ? "

" Plenty of work. Two truck-loads of extra men coming to-morrow."

" Foreigners ? "

" Italians."

I told him the story of a storm at sea with the exaggeration to which one is too prone when addressing simple souls. I rather harrowed him with an account of cook's enamel ware and kitchen things rolling about and jangling when every one was saying his prayers.

Presently I remarked irrelevantly, " My goodness ! What a noise the frogs make here ! "

" That's no noise," said he ; " I'm going to sleep."

After a while his bedfellow came in, and he, before turning in, got down on his knees in the narrow passage between the beds and prayed—I should say, a whole half-hour, talking half to himself, half-aloud. Whilst he. was doing so my bedfellow came in, a tall, heavy, tired Pole, who looked neither to right nor left, but just clambered over me and lay down with his face to the wall and slept and snored.

It rained heavily all night, and next morning it still poured. After a disreputably bad breakfast I sat on a chair at the door of the establishment and watched the thresh of the rain on two great pools beside a road of coal-dust, looked out at the lank grass, the tomato-can dump, the sodden refuse of the boarding-house, and away to the square red chimney of the brick factory belching forth black smoke.

"Say, stranger," said mine host, "I'm going to wade into that cave and hand out potatoes; will you take them from me?" This was the first time I had been called stranger in America, and it sounded pleasant in my ears.

About eleven o'clock in the morning the rain ceased, and I went on to the next point on the railway. The track climbed higher and higher, and I learned that on the morrow I should reach the top of the Alleghany Mountains —Snow Shoe Creek.

It was a fine walk to Orviston under the heavily clouded sky. The mountain-sides were all a-leak with springs and trickling streams and cascades. There was an accompanying music of the racing Beech Creek on the one hand, and of the gushing rivulets on the other; but this would be swallowed up and lost every now and then in the uproar of the oncoming and passing freight train of coal; the appalling, hammering, affrighting freight train passing within two feet of me, taking my breath away with the thought of its power. How pleasant it was, though, to listen to the rebirth of the music of the waters coming to the ear in the wind of the last trucks as they passed.

Orviston prides itself on its fire-bricks. The whole village is made of them, and the pavement as well, and every brick is stamped "Orviston," and is both a commodity and an advertisement.

After I had visited the village store for provisions I re-entered the railway enclosure, and read as I did so the following notice typical of America: " Cultivate the safety habit—if you see anything wrong report it to the man with the button."

I met the man with the button after I had walked a mile along the way ; he was a Slovak, working on the line with pick and shovel, a tall, brawny Slav, and with him a rather tubby little chap of the same nationality.

" You haf no räit on these läins," said the Slovak. " You go off. You are no railway man. What are you ? Slavish ? "

I replied in English, but on second thoughts went on in Russian. He understood, and was mollified at once. He was in America for the second time, they neither of them liked the old country. I photographed them as they stood—John Kresica and Paul Cipriela. They were unmarried men, and lived in a " boarding-house " in Orviston. They worked in a gang. Would I please send them a copy of the photograph ? I agreed to do so ; then, when I moved to go off the lines, the man with the button cried out, smiling :

" Hi ! All-right, go ahead ! "

I went on blithely. There was a change of weather in the afternoon. At one o'clock the sun lifted his arms and pulled apart the mist curtains at the zenith and disclosed himself—a miraculous apparition. The whole sky was cloudy, but the sun was shining. An apparition, the ghost of a sun, and then a reality—hot, light-pouring, cloud-dispersing. By two it was a hot summer day ; at three there was not a cloud in the sky. What a change ! It was clear that summer had progressed during the rain ; insects of bright hues were on the wing, huge yellow-winged butterflies, crimson-thighed grasshoppers, green sun-beetles. A new-born butterfly settled three times on my sleeve ; the fourth time I just caught him. I held him delicately between two fingers and let him go.

During a most exhilarating evening I tramped past houseless Panther and got to Cato at nightfall. Cato was a railway station of no pretensions ; a broken-down shed with no door, no ticket offices, no porter. Passengers who wished to take a train had to wave a flag and trust to the eyesight of the engine-driver. For village, all that I could make out was a coal-bank, a shaft, and some heaps of old iron.

It was an extremely cold night, so I slept in the railway shed on a plank form that ran along the three sides of the building. I lay and looked out at the bright night shining over the mountains, dozed, waked, dozed again. Shortly after midnight I had a strange visitor. I was lying half-asleep, looking at a misshapen star which was resting on the mountains opposite me, which became a silver thumb pointing upward, which became at last the young crescent moon just rising. I was in that somnolent state when you ask, as you see the moon rising behind dark branches of the forest, Is it the moon in eclipse ? is it a comet ?— when a portly man with shovel hat came out of the night, stood in front of the shed, leaned on a thick cudgel, and looked in.

" Hallo ! " said I.

" Haffing sum sleep ? " queried the visitor.

" Yes, trying to ; but it's a cold night."

" Ah, you haf bed pretty goot ! "

" Who are you,—the night watchman ? "

" Naw. You don't see a näit wawtchman without 'is lantern."

The old chap came close up to me, bent down, and whispered, " I'm in the same box as yourself."

" Walking all night ? " I asked.

" The only vay to keep varm," said the old man ruefully. He took out a shining watch from his waistcoat.

"Three o'clock," said he. "In an hour it will be daylight. Oh, I think I'll try and sleep here an hour. Say, is there to eat along the road?"

I wasn't quite sure what he meant.

"Not much," I hazarded.

"Wot are you—you don't speak the langwage very goot," said the tramp.

"English."

"I am a Cherman."

The old man lay down on the plank form, resting his head on my feet, and using them for a pillow.

"How old are ye?" he went on. . . . "Hoh, I can give you forty years. If I were in Germany now I should be getting an army pension."

"Are you going back?" said I.

"Naw, naw. I could never give up this country."

We composed ourselves to sleep, but with his head resting on my feet I was too uncomfortable. "Presently I'll make a fire," said I, "and we'll have hot tea and some bread and butter." And after about twenty minutes I got up, put my boots on, and wandered out to find wood to make a fire. It was about half an hour before dawn. There was a hoar frost, and everything was cold and rimy to the touch. But I made up a bundle of last year's weeds, now sodden straws, and laid them on a half-sheet of my Sunday newspaper. That made a fine blaze, and with twigs and sticks and bits of old plank I soon had a fine bonfire going. The old German came out and watched me incredulously. He didn't think it was possible to make a fire on such a morning. But he was soon convinced, and went about picking up chunks of wood desultorily, alleging the while that he couldn't have lit such a fire in three hours; evidently I knew how to do it.

"Shall I make tea or coffee?" I asked.

"Cawfee," said the old chap, his mouth watering. The word tea did not represent to him anything good.

"After a cup of hot cawfee I can go a long way. Hot cawfee, mind yer. Varm cawfee 'salright for lunch, but in the morning it must be hot. The only thing better than a cup of cawfee is a pint of whisky. . . . Say, you've enough fire here now to roast a chicken."

"Wish I had one; we'd roast it."

I emptied the last of my sugar into the pot, and seven or eight spoonfuls of coffee. It was to be "Turkish." The old tramp sat down on the stump of a tree, took out a curly German pipe, and then put a red coal on it. He had matches, but was economical in the matter of lights. "Say," he said to me later, pointing to the ground, " you've dropped a good match." I picked it up.

The coffee was "real good." The old fellow drank it through his thick moustache, and dipping his bread into his cup, munched great mouthfuls. I had offered him butter with his bread, but he refused. "Booter" was nothing to him. He liked apple-"booter."

"Say, you've got on a powerful pair of boots ! "

"I need them, tramping to Chicago."

"Chicago's not a bad town if you know where to go. Say, presently you'll come to Snow Shoe. Don't go past it. You'll get something there."

The old man stopped a minute in his talk, and stared at me knowingly, didactically.

"Rich miners," he went on. "You need only ask. See this packet of tobacco, they gave it to me at the Company store. That's the thing I can't get on without, must have it. If a man asks me for a smoke and I haf it to give I must give him also. Where've you come from yesterday —Orviston ? "

"No. Monument."

"Is there anything there?" he whispered mysteriously.

"Not much to be had," said I. "But there's a good deal of work, and they're bringing in a big gang of Italians. You can't get much of anything at the farms."

"Where Guineas are, I don't go. I don't like the Eyetaylians."

"D'you like the Jews?"

"They're a good people," said he. "Don't say anything against the Jews. I know a Jew who gives free boots to tramps. Last year I went into his store, and one of the shopmen came up to me and said, 'I know what you want, you'll get it. I'll tell the boss when he comes out.' And he gave me a powerful pair of boots, and sent me across the road to the Quick-lunch with a letter to the boss there, to give me a good dinner. So I never say anything against the Jews."

"Do you know Cleveland?" said I.

"You bet. Lived there ten years ago, had a job on a Lake steamer. I worked one summer on a boat."

The old tramp stared at me as if he had confessed a sin. "Worked like a mule," he added sententiously, and stared again. "I had a home there, and lived just like a married man. But when I wanted to move on to Pittsburg my girl wouldn't go."

"I expect you're the sort of man who has run away from a wife in Germany," said I.

"Naw, naw. Never married."

Then he began to talk of his loves and conquests. At his age you'd have thought his mind would not have been filled with such vanities. He evidently earned money now and then, and went on "sprees." He averred that he had not a dime now, and was altogether "on the nail." I had an idea, however, that he had hidden on him, somewhere, passage-money to take him to Germany, to get that army pension. The Germans are a cautious people. They are cautious and cogitative, yet I wonder what the old man thought of me as he stumped away, leaning on his heavy walking-stick. He had been twenty-seven years on the road, and was very shrewd and experienced in many ways. Perhaps for a moment he took me for a gentleman burglar. He was immensely curious to see what was in my sack, but he probably reflected—" Here is good hot coffee, a fire, and a pleasant young man ; make the most of it, and ask no inconvenient questions."

I put the fire out, shouldered my pack, and resumed the journey to Snow Shoe. The sun had risen, but his warmth was as yet shut away behind the wall of the mountains. The hoar-frost of night had not melted yet, and it was necessary to walk briskly to keep warm. It was so cold that I got to Snow Shoe before ten o'clock.

A feature of this tramping along the rails was the danger in crossing bridges. It was a single line, and as there were some twenty bridges over the flood of the river, there were twenty ordeals of trusting that no train would suddenly appear from a corner of the winding track and run me down. If a train had come whilst I was half-way across a bridge there was no refuge but the river, and I was always prepared to jump. For several nights after this bit of tramping I dreamed of crossing bridges, running on the sleepers and just passing the last beams as engines swept down on me. But it was pleasant climbing up so high, and feeling that within an hour or so Snow Shoe would be achieved. I had lived in the rumour of Snow Shoe for two days, and the name had come to correspond to something very beautiful in my mind. The sound of the name is pleasant to the ear, and every now and then, as I hurried along, I asked, " Snow Shoe, Snow Shoe, what shall I find there ? " I imagined the pioneers who first came up this beautiful valley and gave to an Indian settlement the dainty name—through what virginal loveliness they had passed! Then I thought of the reporter-poet of Scranton who objected to the beauty of Nature because it was independent of man.

Then, man came along, the engine-man, with his endless empty freight train and his bellowing, steaming engine howling through the valley. One after another eight freight trains, each about a quarter of a mile long, came grinding past me, going up to the collieries to take their daily loads of carbon. Somehow I did not object ; it was new America, the America of to-day careering over the America of 1492, and had to be accepted.

But Snow Shoe gave me pause. When I arrived at the little slate-roofed mining settlement I found there was considerable excitement among the children there. A cow had just been cut to pieces by the last freight train. The driver had driven his train over the beast and on without a word of remark or a hesitation, and a farmer was complaining bitterly; but the children—young Americans, Russians, Ruthenians, Slovaks, the ones who have in their keeping the America of to-morrow—were sitting round the remains, helling and God-damning and asking me facetious questions. And that was the answer to what I had asked myself—What shall I see at Snow Shoe ? What am I walking so far and so high for to see ?

Snow Shoe was the dreariest possible mining settlement, and its inhabitants slouched about its coaly ways and in and out of the saloons. Scarcely any one could speak English, and the mines were worked almost exclusively by Poles and Slovaks. The highest point in the Alleghanies, a hand of earth stretched up to heaven, perhaps a maledictory hand.

X.

DECORATION DAY.

AMERICA celebrates no "Whit-Monday," but has
Decoration Day instead; a great national festival,
when medals are pinned on to veterans, the soldiers of the
War of North against South are remembered, and the
graves of heroes are decorated with flags and flowers. On
Decoration Day, and again later, on Independence Day,
the whole populace ceases work in the name of America,
and flocks the streets, sings national songs and hymns,
goes on procession, fires salutes, listens to speeches. We
British are just wildly glad to get free from toil when Whit-
Monday and August Bank Holiday come round. We have
no national or religious fervour on these days. We have
even been known to flock happily to Hampstead and Epping
Forest to the strains of "England's going down the Hill."
Upon occasion the British can be clamorously patriotic,
but only upon occasion. But the American citizen is, to
use his own phrase, "crazy about America" all the while.
The "days-off" that we get are not only off work, but off
everything serious. The American still nurses the hope
with which he came across the ocean, and he is enthusi-
astically attached to the republic he has made and the
principles of that republic.

I spent Decoration Day at Clearfield, a little mining
and agricultural town on the other side of the Alleghanies.
I put up at a hotel for two or three days, and just gave

myself to the town for the time. Early on the festival day
I was out to see how the workaday world was taking things.
All the shops were closed except the ice-cream soda bars
and the fruiterers. There were flags on the banks and
loungers on the streets. Young men were walking about
with flags in their hat ribbons. The cycles and automobiles
on the roadway had their wheels swathed with the stars
and stripes. There were negroes and negresses standing
endimanchés at street corners. Now and then a girl in
white dress and white boots would trip from a house to a
shop and back again. There was an air best expressed
by the words of the song :

> Go along and get yer ready,
>   Get yer glad rags on,
> For there's going to be a meeting
>   In the good old town.

Every town in America is a good old town, and on such
occasions as Decoration Day you may always hear the
worthies of the place giving their reminiscences in the
lounge of a hotel. I sat and listened to many.

We had a very quiet morning, and it seemed to me
there was considerable boredom in the town. There was
a fire in the Opera House about eleven, and I ran behind
the scenes with a crowd of others and stared at the smoking walls. There was a sort of disappointment that the
firemen put it out so promptly.

But after dinner the real holiday commenced, and the
houses began to empty and the streets began to fill. About
four o'clock the " Parade " commenced, what we should
in England call a procession. Every one who owned a
car had it out, carrying roses and ferns and flags. There
was a continual hooting and coughing of motor-horns, and
an increasing buzz of talk. The " Eighth Regimental

Band " appeared, and stood with their instruments in the roadway, chatting to passers-by and being admired. The firemen came with new hats on—their work at the Opera House happily concluded. They now bore on their shoulders wreaths, which were to be carried to the graves of the heroes in the cemetery outside the town. The High School band formed up. A tall man brought a new-bought banner of the Stars and Stripes, which hung from a bird-headed pole. Boy Scouts came in costume—as it were in the rags of the war. The marching order was formed, and then came up what I thought to be the Town Militia, but which turned out to be the representatives of the Mechanics Union, with special decorations and medals on their breasts. The bands began to play ; the automobiles, full of flowers and flags, began to cough and shoot forward ; the flocks of promenaders on the side-walk and in the roadway set themselves to march in step to the festal music. I watched the whole procession, from the Eighth Regimental Band that went first to the eight veterans of the Spanish War, who, with muskets on their shoulders, took up the rear. I stopped several people in the procession and asked them who they were, what exactly was their rôle, for what reason were they decorated with medals,—and every one was glad to satisfy my curiosity. I found that the eight veterans considered themselves technically a squad, and their function was to fire a salute over the graves of the " heroes."

The procession marched round the town to the strains of " Onward, Christian Soldiers " and " O come, all ye faithful." All the people of Clearfield accompanied— Americans, Poles, Ruthenians, Slovaks—for Clearfield has its foreign mining population as well as its Anglo-Saxon urban Americans. As I was going alongside, a young boy ran up and put his hand on my shoulder and addressed me in Polish.

" What's that you say ? " I asked.

" Vairy good ! " said he, and pointed to the procession. " I like it."

" What are you,—Ruthenian, Polish ? " I asked.

" Slavish."

I spoke to him in Russian.

" Oh-ho, he-he, da-da, I thought you were a Polak."

And now he thought I was a Russian ! It touched me rather tenderly. I was dressed like an American, and my attire was not like that of a Russian at all. How enthusiastic this boy was ! It was a real holiday for him. The Slav peoples are emotional ; they need every now and then a means of publicly expressing their feelings. This procession from the town to the graveyard was a link with the customs of their native land, where at least twice a year the living have a feast among the crosses and mounds of the cemetery, and share their joys and interests with the dear dead, whose bodies have been given back to earth.

Among those accompanying the procession were Austrian Slavs, in soot-coloured, broad-brimmed, broken-crowned hats, not yet cast away ; and I noted solemn-faced, placid Russian peasants in overalls staring with half-awakened comprehension. I saw a negro attired in faultless black cloth, having a bunchy umbrella in his hand, a heavy gold chain across his waistcoat, a cigar in his mouth, a soft smoky hat on his head. He tried to get to the front, and I heard one white man say to another, " Make way for him, it's not *your* funeral." The negro is a pretty important person—considering that the war was really fought for him. Perhaps not many actively remember that now ; it is not soothing to do so. It is the American hero who matters more than the cause for which he fell ; though of course America, the idea of America, matters more than either the heroes or the cause. It is a pity that on Decoration

Day there is a tendency to decorate the graves of those who fell in the Spanish War and to pin medals on the survivors of that conflict rather than to perpetuate the memory of the struggle for the emancipation of the negro. America's great problem is the negro whom she has released ; but the Spanish War meant no more than that America's arm proved strong enough to defeat a European power inclined to meddle with her civilisation.

It was, however, at the oldest grave in the cemetery that the procession stopped and the people gathered. All the men were uncovered, and there was a feeling of unusual respect and emotion in the crowd. The wreaths were put down and the flags lowered as the little memorial service commenced. We sang an old hymn, slowly, sweetly, and very sadly, so that one's very soul melted. A hymn of the war, I suppose :

> *Let him sleep,*
> *Calmly sleep,*
> *While the days and the years roll by.*
> *Let him sleep,*
> *Sweetly sleep,*
> *Till the call of the roll on high.*

In the time of the war, in the dark hours of danger and distress, in the times of loss and appalling personal sorrow the Americans were very near and dear to God and to one another—nearer than they are to-day in their peace and prosperity.

When the hymn had been sung, an old grey-headed man came to the foot of the grave and read a portion of the speech made by Abraham Lincoln at the great cemetery at Gettysburg :

Fourscore and seven years ago our fathers brought forth on this continent a new nation conceived in liberty and dedicated to the proposition that all men are created equal. We are now engaged in a great Civil War, testing whether that nation so conceived and so dedicated can long endure. We are met on a great battlefield . . . to dedicate a portion of that field as a final resting-place for those who have given their lives that the nation might live. It is altogether fitting and proper that we should do this.

But in a larger sense we cannot consecrate this ground. The dead themselves have consecrated it. It is rather for us, the living, to consecrate ourselves to the work they died for, that we resolve that these dead shall not have died in vain, that this nation shall have a new birth of freedom and that government of the people, by the people, for the people shall not perish from the earth.

The reading of those words was most impressive. I realised in it the Gospel of America—something more national than even the starry flag.

When the reading was accomplished the eight veterans fired their salute, not up at heaven, but across and over the people's heads, as at an unseen enemy. Then the old grey-headed man who had read the words of Lincoln pronounced the blessing :

The peace of God, which passeth all understanding, keep your hearts and minds in the knowledge and love of God. . . .

And we dispersed to wander among the graves and see the decorations, and add decorations of our own if we willed. Wherever I went, the haunting air was in my ears :

> Let him sleep,
> Sweetly sleep,
> Till the call of the roll on high.

Americans believe very really in the roll-call. They believe that they will answer to their names on a great last day—" When the roll is called up yonder, I'll be there," says a popular hymn. It is all important to the American that he feels he lives and dies for the Right, for the moral virtues. The glory of the wars which the Americans have fought in their history is not only that they, the Americans, were victorious, but that they were morally right before ever they started out to fight.

Well, civilisation has approved the abolition of slavery. The great mass of people nowadays consider slavery as something wrong in itself. The North took up its weapons and convinced the South, and the negro was freed. The peculiar horrors of slavery no longer exist—no one man has power of life and death over the African. That much the war has achieved. But it is strange that for the rest the negro seems to have become worse off, and that America feels that she cannot extend the personal privileges of democracy to the blacks. America has brutalised the nigger; has made of a very gentle, loving and lovable if very simple creature, an outcast, a beast, who may not sit beside an ordinary man. It has in its own nervous imagination accused him of hideous crimes which he did not commit, did not even imagine; it has deprived him of the law, tortured him, flayed him, burned him at the stake. It has made a black man a bogey; so that a fluttering white woman, finding herself alone in the presence of a negro, will rush away in terror, crying " murder," " rape," " fire," just because she has seen the whites of his eyes. Then the hot-blooded southern crowd comes out. . . .

The war was a healthy war. It did much good: it strengthened the roots of many American families; it gave the nation a criterion for future development; it brought many individuals nearer to reality, brought them to the mystery of life, caused them to say each day their prayers to God. But if a war must be judged by its political effect, then as regards the happiness of the negro the war has not yet proved to be a success. The service by the graveside and the apt words of Abraham Lincoln were a reminder to the American people that though they realise to themselves the maximum of prosperity the New World affords, and yet lose their souls, it profits them nothing. America by her unwritten but infallible charter is consecrated to freedom. If America is going to be true to itself it must work for freedom, it must carry out the idea of freedom. The emigrant from Europe expects to realise in America the idea of freedom, the opportunity for personal and individual development. He does not expect to find repeated there the caste system and relative industrial slavery of the East.

．　　　．　　　．　　　．　　　．　　　．

Clearfield was much touched by the graveside service. The whole evening after it the men in the hotel lounge talked American sentiment. The lads and lasses crowded into the cinema houses, and watched with much edification the specially instructive set of films which, on the recommendation of the town council, had been specially installed for the occasion,—the perils of life for a young girl going to dance-halls, the Soudanese at work, Japanese children at play, the ferocious habits of the hundred-legs, a review of troops at Tiflis, a portrait of the Governor of Mississippi wearing a high silk hat, pottery-making in North Borneo, the Pathé news. It was good to see so many pictures of foreign and dark-skinned people presented in an interesting and sympathetic manner. The Americans need to care more for the national life of other races. For they are often strangely contemptuous of the people they conceive to be wasting their time.

I had a pleasant talk with a doctor who was extremely keen on " temperance." He struck up acquaintance with me by complimenting me on my complexion, and betting

I didn't touch spirituous liquors. " The war's still going on," said he. " I wage my part against drink and disease. I'd like to make the medical profession a poor one to enter, yes, sirr. I'd like to uproot disease, and if I could stop the drinking in America I'd do it. Never touch liquor and you'll never have gout, live to a good age, and be happy. I am glad to meet you, sir, glad to meet a Briton. America will stand shoulder and shoulder with the British in war or peace. They are of the same blood. The only two civilised nations in the world."

All the same, Clearfield regarded me with some sus-picion, and as I sat at my bedroom window at night a young man called up :

" English Gawd : Lord Salisbury."

XI.

WAYFARERS OF ALL NATIONALITIES.

THE men whom you meet during the day are like a hand of cards dealt out to you by Providence. But they are more than that, for you feel that luck does not enter into it. You feel there is no such thing as luck, and that the wayfarer is in his way a messenger sent to you by the hospitable spirit of man. He brings a sacred opportunity.

I sit tending my fire, and watching and balancing the kettle upon it ; or I sit beside the cheerful blaze on which I have cooked my breakfast or my dinner, and I hold my mug of coffee in my hand and my piece of bread ; I chip my just-boiled eggs, or I am digging into a pot of apple-jelly or cutting up a pine-apple, and I feel very tender towards the man who comes along the road and stops to pass a greeting and give and take the news of the day and the intelligence of the district.

There is a sort of hermit's charity. It is to have a spirit that is quietly joyful, to be in that state towards man that a gentle woodsman is towards the shy birds who are not afraid of him as he lies on a forest bank and watches them tripping to and from their little nests. Your fellow-man instinctively knows you and trusts you, and he puts aside the mask in which he takes refuge from other fellow-travellers who are alert and busy. I cherish as very pre-

cious all the little talks I had with this man and that man
who came up to me in America.

As I sat one day by the side of my pleasant Susquehanna road, an oil-carrier met me, a gentle-voiced man
in charge of four tons of kerosene and petrol, which his
horses were dragging over the mountains from village to
village and store to store. It was an opportunity to rest
the horses, and the driver pulled up, relaxed his reins and
entered into converse with me. Was I going far? Why
was I tramping? What nationality was I? I told him
what I was doing, and he said he would like to give up his
job and do the same; he also was of British origin, though
his mother was a German. He was a descendant of Sir
Robert Downing. "There used to be many English about
here," said he, "but they wore off." He went on to tell
me what a wild district it had once been. His grandfather
had shot a panther on the mountains. But there were no
panthers now. The railways and the automobiles had
frightened the wild things away. The change had come
about very suddenly. He remembered when there were
no telephone-poles along the road, but only road-poles.
It used to be a posting-road, and a good one too ; but now
the automobiles had torn up all the surface, and no one
would take any trouble about the needs of horse vehicles.

One hot noontide, on the road to Shippenville and Oil
City, I was having luncheon when a very pleasant Swede
came down the road carrying a bucket in his hand,—Mr.
G. B. Olson, bossing a gang of workers on the highway.
He was going down the hill to a special spring to draw
water for his thirsty men, but he could hardly resist the
smoke of my wayside fire, and he told me, as it seemed, his
whole story. He had come to America in 1873, and had
worked on a farm in Illinois before the great Chicago fire.
He was twenty-four then, and was sixty-five now.

When he heard I was British he told me how he had come from Europe *via* Leith and Glasgow, and had been fifteen and a half days crossing the Atlantic.

" Have you ever been back to Sweden ? " I asked.

" No, sirr, never."

" Are you content with America ? "

" Yes, sirr ; it's the finest country under the sun. It gives the working man a show."

" The Americans speak very kindly of your countrymen. They like them."

" Yes. We gave the Americans a good lift, we Swedes, Norwegians, Danes, and Germans, by settling the land when the rest of the colonists were running to the towns. We came in and did the rough pioneer work that had to be done if America was going to be more than a mushroom growth. Where would America be to-day if it were not for us in Minnesota, Wisconsin, Iowa ? You can't keep up big cities unless you've got plenty of men working in the background on the land."

The Swede went on to compliment me on my English. I spoke pretty clear for one who had been only three months in the country. He had met many British who spoke " very broken," especially Scotch. " I shouldn't have been able to understand them," said he, " but that I am a foreigner myself, and know what it is not to speak good."

" Well, I must be off," he added, and pointed to the bucket.

" You've got a gang of men working up above ? "

" Yes. I'm bossing them for the State. A good job it is too, good money, and I don't have to work much."

" I should say you'd make a kind boss ! "

" Yes. I never do anything against them. I get a good day's work out of the men, but I never put myself above them. I've got authority, that's all—it doesn't make

6

me better'n they. I've got to boss them, they've got to
work. That's how it's turned out. . . . . Well, I must be
off to water my hands!"

And he hastened away down the hill, whilst I put my
things together and shouldered my pack.

The strange thing about this American journey was the
diversity of nationality I encountered, and the friendly
terms in which it was possible for me as a man on the road
to converse with them.

On leaving Clearfield I fell in with Peter Deemeff, a clever
little Bulgarian immigrant, and spent two days in his company. He was an unpractical, rebellious boy, a student
by inclination, but a labourer by necessity, nervous in
temperament, and alternately gay and despondent. He
was thin-bodied, broad-browed, clean-shaven, but blue-
black with the multitude of his hair-roots; he had two
rows of faultless, little milk-white teeth, an angelic Bulgarian smile, and an occasional ugly American grimace.

We tramped along the most beautiful Susquehanna
road to Curwenville, and then through magnificent gorges
to the height of Luthersburg.

"Ho! Where are you going?" said one of a group of
Italian labourers at Curwenville.

"Oil City," I answered.

"You'll be sore," the Italian rejoined, and slapped his
thigh. "Why not stop here and get good job?"

But Peter and I were not looking for a job just then,
and we went on. I was glad the Bulgarian was not tempted,
for I relished his company, and he was pleasantly loqua-
cious.

"Do you like the Americans?" I asked him.

He raised his eyebrows. Evidently he did not like them
very much.

"Half-civilise," said he. "When I say my boss, 'I go,'

he want me fight. He offens me. I say, ' You Americans
—bulldogs, no more, half-civilise.' And I go all the same
and no fight great big fat American."

" You think Bulgaria a better country ? "

" 'S a poor country, that's all. There's more life in
Europe. Americans don't know what they live for."

I looked with some astonishment on this day-labourer
in shabby attire talking thus intelligently, and withal so
frankly.

He told me he hated the English. They had said,
anent the Balkan War, " The fruits must not be taken from
the victors " ; but when Montenegro took Scutari they
were the first to say to King Nicholas, " Go back, go back."
He thought I was a Slav immigrant like himself, or he would
not have struck up acquaintance with me. But he seemed
relieved when I told him my sympathies were entirely with
the Slavs.

We talked of Russian literature, and of Tolstoy in particular.

" Tolstoy understood about God," said he. " He said
God is within you, not far away or everywhere, but in yourself. By that I understand life. All life springs from
inside. What comes from outside is nahthing. That is
how Americans live—in outside things, going to shows,
baseball matches. . . . I know Shakespeare was the mirror
of life, that's not what I mean. . . . To be educated mentally is light and life ; to be developed only physically
is death and . . . That's why I say bulldogs, not civi-
lise. When I was in Philadelphia I hear a Socialist in the
Park and he asked, ' How d'ye fellows live ?—eat—work,
eat—work—drink, eat—work—sleep, eat—work—sleep.
Machines, that's what y'are.' "

The most astonishing evidence of thought and culture
that Peter Deemeff gave me was contained in a reflection

he made half-aloud, in a pause in the conversation—"A great writer once said, ' If God had not existed, man would have invented his God '—that is a good idea, eh ? " Fancy that from the lips of an unskilled labourer ! These foreign working-men are bringing something new to America. If they only settle down to be American citizens and look after their children's education !

" Do many Bulgarians think ? " I asked him.

" Yes, many—they think more than I do."

We spent the night under great rocks ; he under one, I under another. My bed, which I made soft with last year's bracken, was under three immense boulders, a natural shelter, a deep dark cavern with an opening that looked across the river-gorge to the forested cliff on the other side. The Bulgarian, less careful about his comfort, lay in a ferny hollow, just sheltered by an overhanging stone. Before lying down he commended himself to God, and crossed himself very delicately and trustfully. With all his philosophy he had not cast off the habits of the homeland. And almost directly he laid himself down he fell asleep.

It was a wonderful night. As I lay in my cave and the first star was looking down at me from over the great wooded cliff, what was my astonishment to see a living spark go past the entrance of the cave, a flame on wings— the firefly. I lay and watched the forest lose its trees, and the cliff become one great black wall, ragged all along the crest. Mists crept up and hid the wall for a while, and then passed. An hour and a half after I had lain down, and the Bulgarian had fallen asleep, I opened my eyes and looked out at the black wall—little lamps were momentarily appearing and disappearing far away in the mysterious dark depths of the cliff. It seemed to me that if when we die we perish utterly, then that living flame moving past my door was something like the passing of man's life. It was strange to lie on the plucked rustling bracken, and have the consciousness of the cold sepulchre-like roof of the cave, and look out at the figure of man's life. But the river chorus lulled me to sleep. Whenever I reawakened and looked out I saw the little lights once more, appearing and vanishing, like minutest sprites searching the forest with lanterns.

Peter and I woke almost at the same time in the morning in a dense mist. I sent him for water, and I collected wood for a fire. We made tea, took in warmth, and then set off once more.

"Let us go to a farm-house and get some breakfast," said I.

"We get it most likely for nothing, because it's Sunday," said Peter, with a smile.

The Americans are much more hospitable on Sundays than on week-days. They do not, however, like to see you tramping the road on the day of rest; it is thought to be an infraction of the Sabbath—though it is difficult to see what tramps can do but tramp on a Sunday.

We had a splendid breakfast for ten cents apiece at a stock-breeding farm below Luthersburg,—pork and beans, bread and butter and cookies, strawberry jam and home-canned plums, pear-jelly. I thanked the lady of the establishment when we had finished, and remarked that I thought it very cheap at the price. She answered that she didn't serve out lunches for a profit, but wouldn't let decent men pass hungry.

"Are you hiking to the next burg?" she asked.

"Chicago," said I.

"Gee!"

We came to Luthersburg, high up on the crest of the hills, a large village, with two severe-looking churches.

"When I see these narrow spires I'm afraid," said the Bulgarian. "I should have to wither my soul and make it small to get into one of these churches. I like a church with walls of praise and a spire of yearning,—Tolstoy, eh ? That spire says to me, ' I feared Thee, O God, because Thou art an austere man.' "

I, for my part, thought it strange that Americans, taking so many risks in business, and daring and imagining so large-heartedly in the secular world, should be satisfied with so cramped an expression of their religion.

Peter and I went down on the other side of the hills to Helvetia, the first town in a wild coaling district, a place of many Austrians, Poles, and Huns. It was the Sunday evening promenade, and every one was out of doors, hundreds of miners and labourers in straight-creased trousers (how soon obtained) and cheap felt hats, a similar number of dark, interesting-looking Polish girls in their gaudy Sunday best. We passed a hundred yards of grey coke-ovens glowing at all their doors and emitting hundreds of fires and flames. Peter seemed unusually attracted by the coke-ovens or by the Slav population, and he decided to remain at Helvetia and seek for a job on the morrow. So I accompanied him into a " boarding-house," and was ready to spend the night with him. But when I saw the accommodation of coaly beds I cried off. So the Bulgarian and I parted. I went on to Sykesville and the Hotel Sykes. Obviously I was in America,—fancy calling a hotel in England " Hotel Sykes." But I did not stay there, preferring to hasten up country and get a long step beyond black breaker-towers, the sooty inclines up which trucks ran from the mines, the coke-ovens, the fields full of black stumps and rotting grass, the seemingly poverty-stricken frame-buildings, and more dirt and misery than you would see even in a bad district in Russia. It surprised me to see the Sunday clothes of Sykesville, the white collars, the bright red ties, the blue serge trousers with creases, the bowler hats, and American smiles. Despite all the dirt, these new-come immigrants say *Yes* to American life and American hopes. But to my eyes it was a terrible place in which to live. It was an astonishing change, moreover, to pass from the magnificent loveliness of the Susquehanna gorges to this inferno of a colliery. But I managed to pass out of this region almost as quickly as I came into it, and next day was in the lovely country about Reynoldsville; and I tramped through beautiful agricultural or forested country to the bright towns of Brookville, Clarion, and Shippenville, clean, new, handsome settlements, with green lawns, shady avenues, fine houses, and well-stocked shops. In such places I saw America at its best, just as at Helvetia and Sykesville I saw it at about its worst. I suppose Sykesville will never be made as beautiful as Brookville ; the one is the coal-cellar, the other is the drawing-room in the house of modern America.

But I had definitely left the coal region behind ; now I was striking north, for oil. In three days I came into Oil City, so wonderfully situated on the wide and stately Alleghany river—the river having brown rings here and there, glimmering with wandering oil. The city is built up five or six hills, and is only a unity by virtue of its fine bridges. It is a clean town compared with Scranton, as oil is cleaner to deal with than coal. But the houses are more ramshackle. The poor people's dwellings suggest to the eye that they were made in a great hurry many years ago, and are now falling to bits ; they are set one behind another up the hills, and you climb to them by wooden stairways. Some seem veritably tumbling down the hill. There were a fair number of foreign immigrants there, mostly Italians ; but the oil business seems to be worked by Americans, the foreigners being too stupid to understand. Oil City is a cheap town to live in. I was boarded at a hotel for a dollar a day ; and when I bought provisions for my next tramp to Erie Shore I found everything cheaper than in Eastern Pennsylvania. There appeared to be little cultured life, however, no theatre but the cinema, and little offered for sale in the shape of books.

I set out for Meadville on the " Meadville Pike." A feature of the new landscape and of the road and fields was the oil-pump, working all by itself, the long cables, connecting the pump with the engine, often coming across the roadway, the *jig, jig, jig* of the pumping movement, the *clump, clump, clump, stump* of the engine—the pulse of the industrial countryside.

I met a Dutchman.   He asked :

" What's on ?   What is it for ? "

I told him I was studying the emerging American, and he told me what a menace the fecund Slavs were to the barren Americans.   According to him the extinction of the American was a matter of mathematics.

I came upon an enormous gang of Americans, Russians, Slavs, Italians at work on the high road, digging it out, laying a bed of mortar, putting down bricks ; some hundreds of workmen, extending over a mile and a half of closed road.   Many of the American workmen were dressed as smartly as stockbrokers' clerks and city men, and they kept themselves neat and clean—a new phenomenon in labouring.   Americans, however, were working together, Italians together, and Russians together.   A fine-looking American workman said to me knowingly, " You can photograph me if you like, but the Guineas won't want to be photographed—most of them shot some one sometime or other, you bet ! "

Near Cochranton I made the acquaintance of five little girls—Julia, Margaret, Elinor, Cora, and Georgiana—scampering about in bare legs and week-day frocks, whilst father and mother, with gauze bags on their heads, were " boxing the bees." It was the first swarm of summer ; two lots of bees had been boxed, but the third was giving much trouble. Julia, aged twelve, was a very pretty girl, and when at her mother's recommendation she went indoors, washed her face and put on a Sunday frock, she looked a very smart young lady. She was conscious of that fact, and informed me in course of conversation that she was going to travel when she was grown up. She was dying to see Paris, and she wanted to visit all the European towns !

Some miles north, near Frenchville, I met one of the French colonists of Northern Pennsylvania,—a tall, well-built stripling,—and he told me how the Breton peasants had settled at Boussot and Frenchville, bringing all their French ways of farming and economy, and becoming the admiration of the district around—a little Brittany. The young man's father-in-law had been the first Frenchman to come and settle in the district. After him had come, straight from France, relatives and friends, and relatives of friends and friends of friends in widening circles. They were beginning to speak English well now, but the new-comers were still without the new language. It was in-teresting for me to realise what a great gain such people were to America—to the American nation in the making. It is good to think of such agricultural settlements lying in the background of industrial America—the whole villages of Swedes, of Russians, of Danes, Finns, Germans, French. They are ethnic reserves ; they mature and improve in the background. They are Capital. If urban America can subsist on the interest, the surplus of the ambitious, how much richer she will be than if the population of whole country-sides is tempted to rush *pêle-mêle* to the places of fortune-making and body-wasting.

Coming into Meadville, a town of twelve thousand inhabitants, most of the labourers of whom are Italians employed at the great railway works, I was attracted to Nicola Hiagg, a Syrian, sitting outside his ice-cream shop reading the Syrian paper. Whilst I had a "pine-apple soda," I drew him into talk. It was a matter of pleasing interest to him that I had myself tramped in Syria, and knew the conditions in his native land. Nicola had first left Syria twelve years ago, had come to Philadelphia, and started making his living selling "soft drinks" in the street. After five years he had saved enough to take a holiday and go back to the old land. He and his brother had been merchants in Jerusalem before he set out for America; the brother had had charge of the store, and Nicola had convoyed the merchandise and the train of thirty asses to and from the country. He had many friends in Syria, but it was a poor country. The Turks were blood-suckers, and drained it of every drop of vital energy.

"I lived in a poor little town between Beyrout and Damascus, not with my brother in Jerusalem. So poor! You cannot start anything new in Syria—the Turk inter-teres. No bizness! What you think of the war? The Turk is beaten, hey? Now is the time for the Syrians to unite and throw off the Turk. There are Syrians all over the world; they are prosperous everywhere but in Syria. . . . America is a fine country; but if Syria became in-dependent I'd go back. . . ."

Nicola, when he had his holiday, found a Syrian girl and brought her back to America as his wife. She was not visible now, however; for the Syrian kept her in the back-ground, and he told me he didn't believe in women's rights to public life. A bit of a Turk himself!

He was very proud of his little girl, who is being brought up as an American in the town school. "Already she can write, and when you say to her, ' Write something,' she does not look up at you and say, ' How d'you spell it ? ' She just writes it."

" She's sharp."

" You bet."

The Turks, the Greeks, and the Syrians, and to some extent the Italians, are engaged in the sweet-stuff and ice-cream business. Turkish Delight, the most characteristic thing of the Levant, seems to be their bond of union. It is a great business in America, for the Americans are, beyond all comparison, fonder of sweet things than we are. I stopped one day at a great candy shop in South Bend, Indiana. It was kept by a Mr. Poledor, who was so pleased that I had been in Greece and knew the habits of the Greek Orthodox, that he gave me the freedom of the shop and bade me order anything I liked—he would " stand treat." There were over a hundred ways of having ice-cream, twenty sorts of ice-cream soda, thirteen sorts of lemonade, twelve frappés, and the menu card was something like a band programme. Mr. Poledor was a man of inventiveness, and the names of some of the dishes were as delicious as the dishes themselves.   I transcribe a few :

> Merry Widow.
> Don't Care.
> John D. (is very rich).
> Yankee Doodle.
> Upside down.
> New Moon.
> Sweet Smile.
> Twin Beauties.
> Nôtre Dame.
> Lover's Delight.
> Black-eyed Susan.

A young man could take his girl there and give her

anything she asked for, were it the moon itself. The Greek was a magician.

But to return. As I was going out of Meadville, two young men swung out of a saloon and addressed me thus strangely :

" Have you had a benevolent ? We're giving them away."

One of them showed me a stylographic pen.

" Wha're you doing ? " said the other.

" Oh, I'm travelling," I replied.

" How d'ye get your living ? "

" I write in the magazines now and then."

A look of disappointment crept over the faces of the young men. The stylographic pen was replaced in waist-coat pocket.

" Did you say you were working for a magazine ? So are we—*The Homestead*. I was about to ask you to become a subscriber."

" And the benevolent ? " I asked.

" Oh, these are given away to subscribers."

I explained that I wasn't a commercial traveller, but one of those who wrote sometimes in magazines.

" You'd be a sort of reporter ? "

" Well, not quite."

" A poet ? "

" No. I earn my living by writing."

" Better than a poet, I suppose. Well, good-day, wish you luck ! "

So I won free of my last big town in mighty Penn-sylvania, and set out for the State of Ohio.

I had a " still-creation-day " in quiet country, and to-wards evening came through the woods to the store and house of Padan-Aram. And just on the border of Ohio an elf-like person skipped out of a large farm and conducted me across, a boy of about twenty years, who cried out to me shrilly as he caught me up :

" I say, you're still in Pennsylvania."

" Yes," said I.

" Yes, but that house over there is in Ohio. Say! Would you like some candy ? "

" I thought you were fumbling in your pocket for tobacco," said I.

" No use for it," said the boy. " I've found God. I used to chew it, but I've stopped it."

" That is good. You've a strong will," said I.

" I reckon God can break any will," said the boy. " Once I ran away from home with five hundred dollars. You're walking ? I can walk. I walked a hundred miles in five days and five nights. Feet were sore for a week. Five times I ran away. The sixth time I stayed away four years and worked on the steel works."

" Were your parents unkind ? " I asked. " Or did you run away to see life ? "

" Ran to show them I could," said the boy. " They lay in to me, I can tell you. There were Chinamen and niggers —all sorts. Hit a fellow over the head with an ice-cream refrigerator—killed him dead."

" Where was this ? "

" Poke. At the institution. I showed them I could fight."

" What are you, American ? "

" Pennsylvanian Dutch."

" I suppose there is a church about here that you go to ? "

" Yes ; a Methodist. But I don't go. Family service. We get many blessings."

" Is there a hotel at Padan-Aram ? "

" No ; but at Leon. If you go there, you'll get a

Christian woman. You'll find God. She'll lighten your load. She's a saint. I know her well."

" What's your name ? I'll mention you to her."

" Dull."

" I'll tell her I met you."

" Tell her you met Ralph Dillie—she'll know."

" All right," said I.

" Now you're in Ohio," said the boy. " Are you going into the store at Padan-Aram ? "

" No."

" Don't you want to buy some candy ? "

" No. I don't eat it along the road."

" Buy some for me."

" All right ; yes."

" Buy a nickel's worth."

" Yes."

Ralph Dillie rejoiced. We went into the store and ordered a nickel's worth of candy. And directly the boy got it he started back for home on the run. And I watched him re-cross the border once more—into Pennsylvania.

XII.

CHARACTERISTICS.

THE chief characteristic of America is an immense patriotism, and out of that patriotism spring a thousand minor characteristics, which, taken by themselves, may be considered blemishes by the critical foreigner,— such troublesome little characteristics as national pride and thin-skinnedness, national bluster and cock-sureness. But personal annoyance should not blind the critic or appreciator to the fundamental fact of the American's belief in America. This belief is not a narrow partizanship, though it may seem unpleasantly like that to those who listen to the clamour of excited Americans at the Olympic games and other competitions of an international interest. It is not merely the commercial instinct ever on the watch for opportunities for self-advertisement. It is a real, hearty patriotic fervour, the deepest thing in an American. It is something that cannot be shaken.

" *It is a sacrament to walk the streets as an American citizen,*" says a Presbyterian circular. " *Being an American is a sacred mission. Our whole life must be enthralled by a holy passion.*"

You could never hear it said, except in an imperial way, that being a Briton, or being a German, or being a Russian was a sacred mission. In Britain it would be bad form, in Germany absurd, in Russia quite untrue. It is part of the greatness of America that she can come forward unashamed and call herself the handmaiden of the Lord.

Now there is a fine healthy spirit abroad in the land counteracting the more sentimental and sanctimonious self-honour of the Americans. Something more in deeds than in words, a pulse that beats for America, a greater purpose that breathes through myriads of personal acts, done for personal ends. Outside, beyond the degrading commercialism of the nation, there is a feeling that building for a man is building also for America ; that buying and selling in the store is buying and selling for the great nation ; that writing or singing or painting, though done in self-conceited cities and before limited numbers, is really all consecrated to the idea of the new America.

In several schools of America the children take the following pledge :

I am a citizen of America and an heir to all her greatness and renown. The health and happiness of my own body depend upon each muscle and nerve and drop of blood doing its work in its place. So the health and happiness of my country depend upon each citizen doing his work in his place.

I will not fill any post or pursue any business where I can live upon my fellow-citizens without doing them useful service in return ; for I plainly see that this must bring suffering and want to some of them. I will do nothing to desecrate the soil of America, or pollute her air or degrade her children, my brothers and sisters.

I will try to make her cities beautiful, and her citizens healthy and happy, so that she may be a desired home for myself now, and for her children in days to come.

Teachers are recommended to explain to children that patriotism means love of your own country and not hate of other countries ; and that the best mode of patriotism is love and care for the ideals of the fatherland.

The most obvious fields of activity are the school, the building, the yard or playgrounds, and the surrounding streets.

Whatsoever is offensive and unsightly, detrimental to health, or in violation of law, is a proper field for action. The litter of papers and refuse ; marks on side walks, buildings, and fences ; mutilation, vandalism, and damage of any kind to property ; cleanliness of the school building and the surrounding streets, door-yards, and pavements ; observance of the ordinances for the disposal of garbage by the scavenger and people in the community ; protection and care of shade trees ; improper advertisements, illegal signs and bill-boards ; unnecessary noises in the streets around the school, including cries of street-vendors and barking of dogs and blowing of horns ; the display of objectionable pictures and postcards in the windows of stores—all supply opportunities to the teachers to train pupils for good citizenship.

Circulars like the following are scattered broadcast to citizens, and they breathe the patriotism of the American :

Do you approve of your Home City ?

I mean, do you like her looks, her streets, her schools, her public buildings, her stores, factories, parks, railways, trolleys, and all that makes her what she is ? Do you approve of these things as they are ? Do you think they could be better ? Do you think you know how they can be made better ?

If you do you are unusual. Few take the trouble to approve or disapprove. Many may think they care about the city ; but few, very few, act as if they did !

When you see something you think can be improved you go straight and find out who is the man who has that something in charge ; whatever it is, factories, smoke, stores, saloons, parks, paving, playgrounds, lawns, backyards, ash-cans, overhead signs, newspapers, bill-boards, side-walks, street cars, street lighting, motor traffic, freight yards, or what not, you find out who is the man who has in charge that thing you dislike ; then you talk to him, or write to him, and tell him what you disapprove of, and ask him if he can and will make it better, or tell you why he can't. He wants to make it better.

He will if he can. Almost invariably he wants to do his work of looking after that thing better than it was ever done before. He will welcome your complaint; he will explain his handicaps; he will ask your help. Then you give the help.

J. C. D.

Making the city beautiful and fostering a love for the home-city, however dingy and dreary that city may at present be, is one of the most potent and attractive expressions of American patriotism, and it is well to note the characteristic. It has great promise for the America of the future, the America which the sons and daughters of the immigrants will inherit. The America of the future is to be one of artistically imagined cities and proud, responsible citizens. Even now, despite the unlovely state of New York and Chicago and the reputation for devastating ugliness which America has in Europe, there are clear signs of the commencement of an era of grace and order. Already the parks of the American cities are the finest in the world, and are worth much study in themselves. American townsmen have loved Nature enough to plant trees so that every decent town on the western continent has become a cluster of shady avenues. Some cities favour limes, some maples; New Haven is known as "The City of Elms"; in Washington alone it is said that there are 78,000 street trees; Cleveland has been called "The City of the Forest." Wherever I tramped in America I found the most delicious shade in the town streets—excepting, of course, the streets of the coaling infernos of Pennsylvania. No idea of the expense of land deters the American from getting space and greenery into the midst of his wilderness of brick and mortar. It is said that the value of the parks in such a city as Newark, for instance, is over two and a quarter millions of pounds (nine million dollars). "Our aim," says a Newark circular, "is the city beautiful, and it requires the aid of everyday patriots to make it so. Pericles said, ' Make Athens beautiful, for beauty is now the most victorious power in the world.' "

America has become the place of continuous crusades—against dirt, against municipal corruption, immorality, noise. It would surprise many Europeans to know the fight which is being made against bell-advertisement, steam whistles, organ-grinders' music, shouts of street hawkers, and the exuberance of holiday-makers.

" Don't be ashamed to fight for your city to get it clean and beautiful, to rid it of its sweat-shops and hells," I read in a Chicago paper. " Some folk call our disease Chicago-itis, but that is a thousand times better than Chicagophobia. Those suffering from Chicagophobia are as dangerous to society as those who have hydrophobia."

Then, most potent expression of all in American patriot-ism is the American's belief in the future of its democracy, the faith which is not shattered by the seeming bad habits of the common people, the flocking to music-halls and cinema shows, the reading of the yellow press.

It has been noted in the last few years that there is a distinct falling off in the acceleration of reading at the public libraries. This is attributed to the extraordinary amount of time spent by men and women at the " movies," when they would otherwise be reading. Such a fact would breed pessimism in Great Britain or Europe were it estab-lished. But America has such trust in the hearts and hopes of the common people that it approves of the picture show. " If readers of books go back to the cinema, let them go," says the American ; " it is like a child in the third class voluntarily going back to the first class, because the work being done there is more suited to his state of mind." The cinema show is doing the absolutely elementary work among the vast number of immigrants, who are almost illiterate. It is not a be-all and an end-all, but stimulates the mind and sets it moving, thinking, striving. The picture show will bring good readers to the libraries in time. It is the first step in the cultural ladder of the democracy.

Then people of good taste in Europe decry the reading of newspapers ; a leader of thought and politics like A. J. Balfour can boast that he never reads the papers. But America says, " You have the newspaper habit. This habit is one of the most beneficial and entertaining habits you have. Few people read too many newspapers. Most people do not read enough." This, of American papers of all papers in the world. But let me go on quoting the most significant words of America's great librarian, J. Cotton Dana :

Readers of newspapers are the best critics of them. The more they are read the wiser the readers ; the wiser the readers the more criticisms, and the more the newspapers are criticised the better they become.

Do you say this does not apply to the yellow journal ? I would reply that it does. The yellow journal caters all the time to the beginners in reading, who are also the beginners in newspaper reading. A new crop of these beginners in reading is born every year. This new crop likes its reading simply printed, in large letters, and with plenty of pictures. The more of this new crop of readers there are the more the yellow journals flourish ; and the more the yellow journals flourish the sooner this new crop is educated by the yellow journals, by the mere process of reading them, and the sooner they get into the habit of reading journals that are not yellow and contain a larger quantity of more reliable information, until at last the yellow journals are overpassed by the readers they have themselves trained.

The yellow press is the second rung on the cultural ladder of democracy. America is glad of it, glad also of the princess novelette, the pirate story, glad of Hall Caine and Marie Corelli ; all these are, as it were, divining-rods for better things. The American says " Yes " to the novels of Florence Barclay, as indeed most sensible Britons would also. *The Rosary* was a most helpful book—so much more helpful to the unformed intellect and young intelligence of the mass of the people than, for instance, Tolstoy's dangerously overpraised *Resurrection* or Wells's *New Machiavelli*. America recognises the truth that the ugly has power to make those who look at it ugly like itself ; but that the crude and elementary stuff, however poor it may be artistically, is nevertheless most useful to democracy if it speaks in language and sentiment which is common knowledge to the reader. How useful to America is such a book as Churchill's *Inside of the Cup*.

It is a very true dictum that " reading makes more reading " ; and in a young, hopeful nation, striving to divine its own destiny and to visualise its future, " more reading " always means *better reading*.

Perhaps the cultured ladder of democracy may be seen allegorically as the ladder of Jacob's dream. Religion, which may be thought to have flown from the churches, is in evidence at the libraries. It is a librarian who is able to say in *The Inside of the Cup* that we are on the threshold of a greater religious era than the world has ever seen.

In America to-day we are confronted with two parties,— one the great multifarious, unformed mass of the people, and the other the strong, emancipated, cultured American nation, which is at work shaping the democracy. The aspect of the " rabble," the commercial heathen, and horde of unknowing, unknown immigrants, gives you the first but not the final impression of America. You remark first of all the slouching, blank-eyed, broad-browed immigrant, who indulges still his European vices and craves his European pleasures, flocking into saloons, debauching his body, or at best looking dirty and out of hand, a reproach to the American flag.   You see the Jews leaping over one another's backs in the orgy of mean trade.   You see the fat American, clever enough to bluff even the Jew—the strange emerging bourgeois type of what I call the " white nigger," low-browed, heavy-cheeked, thick-lipped, huge-bodied, but *white ;* men who seem made of rubber, so elastic they are ; men who seem to get their thoughts from below upward. I've often watched one of these " white negroes " reflecting ; he seems to sense his thoughts in his body first of all—you can watch his idea rise up to him from the earth, pass along his body, and flicker at last in a true American smile across his lips—a transition type of man, I should say. One wonders where these men, who are originally Jews or Anglo-Saxons or Dutch or Germans, got their negro souls. It would almost tempt one to think that there were negro souls floating about, and that they found homes in white babies.

Beside the fat American is the more familiar lean, hatchet-faced type, which is thought to correspond to the Red Indian in physiognomy.   Perhaps too much importance is attached to the Darwinian idea that the climate of America is breeding a race of men with physique and types similar to the aborigines.   The American is still a long way from the red-skin.   Meanwhile, however, one may note with a smile the extraordinary passion of Americans for collecting autographs, curios, snippets of the clothes of famous men, Italian art, British castles,—which seems to be scalp-hunting in disguise.   The Americans are great scalp-hunters.

On the whole, the dry, lean Americans are the most trustworthy and honourable among the masses of the people. In England we trust fat men, men "who sleep o' nights," but in America one prefers the lean man. Shakespeare would not have written of Cassius as he did if he had been an American of to-day. Of course too much stress might easily be laid on the unpleasantness of the "white-nigger" type. There are plenty of them who are true gentlemen.

The American populace has also its bad habits. There are those who chew "honest scrap," and those who chew "spearmint." It is astonishing to witness the service of the cuspidor in a hotel, the seven or eight obese, cow-like American men, all sitting round a cuspidor and chewing tobacco ; almost equally astonishing to sit in a tramcar full of American girls, and see that every jaw is moving up and down in the mastication of sweet gum.

America suffers terribly from its own success, its vastness, its great resources, its commercial scoops, its wealth, vested *en masse* and so vulgarly in the person of lucky or astute business men. This has bred a tendency to chronic exaggeration in the language of the common people ; it has brought on the jaunty airs and tall talk of the man who, however ignorant he may be, thinks that he knows all. But success has also brought kindness and an easy-going temperament. There are no people in the world less disposed to personal ill-temper than the Americans. They are very generous, and in friendship rampageously exuberant. They are not mean, and are disinclined to incur or to collect small debts. They would rather toss who pays for the drinks of a party than pay each his own score. They have even invented little gambling machines in cigar stores and saloons where you can put a nickel over a wheel and run a chance between having five cigars for five cents, or paying twenty-five cents for no cigars at all.

So stands on the one hand the "many-headed," sprung

from every country in Europe, an uncouth nation doing what they ought not to do, and leaving undone what they ought to do, but at least having in their hearts, every one of them, the idea that America is a fine thing, a large thing, a wonderful promise. Opposite them stands what may be called the American *intelligence*, ministering as best it can to the wants of young America, and helping to fashion the great desideratum,—a homogeneous nation for the new world.

It seems perhaps a shame to question the significance of any of the phenomena of American life of to-day, to tie what may be likened to a tin can to the end of this chapter ; but I feel that this is the most fitting place to put a few notes which I have made of tendencies which are apt to give trouble to the mind of Europeans otherwise very sympathetic to America and America's ideal. They are quite explicable phenomena, and in realising and understanding them for himself the reader will be enabled to get a truer idea of the atmosphere of America.

On my way into Cleveland I read in the *Pittsburg Post* the following statistics of life at Princetown College, of the students at the College :

184 men smoke.
  76 began after entering College, but 51 students have stopped smoking since entering College.
  91 students wear glasses, and 57 began to wear them since entering.
  15 students chew tobacco.
  19 students consider dancing immoral.
  16 students consider card-playing immoral.
206 students correspond with a total of 579 girls.
203 students claim to have kissed girls in their time.
  24 students have proposed and been rejected.

Another day I read in the *New York American* the story of the adventures of Watts's " Love and Life " in America :

The peripatetic painting, " Love and Life," the beautiful allegorical work, by George Frederick Watts, once more reposes in an honoured niche in the White House. The varied career of this painting in regard to White House residence extends over seventeen years.

This picture, painted in 1884, was presented to the national Government by Watts as a tribute of his esteem and respect for the United States, and was accepted by virtue of a special act of Congress. This was during the second administration of President Cleveland, and he ordered it hung in his study on the second floor of the White House. Two replicas were made by Watts of the painting, and one was placed by the National Art Gallery, London, and the other in the Louvre, Paris.

The two figures of " Love and Life " are entirely nude, and the publication of reproductions awoke the protests of purists who circulated petitions to which they secured hundreds of names to have it removed to an art gallery. Finally, the Clevelands yielded to the force of public opinion, and sent the offending masterpiece to the Corcoran Art Gallery.

When Theodore Roosevelt became President he brought the art exile back to the White House. The hue and cry arose again, and he sent it back to the Gallery, only to bring it back again toward the close of his administration to hang in the White House once more.

The Tafts, failing to see the artistic side of the painting, had it carried back to the Gallery.

There it seemed destined to stay. The other day Mrs. Woodrow Wilson, accompanied by her daughter Eleanor, both artists of merit, toured the Corcoran Art Gallery. They were shown " Love and Life," and told the tragic story of its wanderings.

Mrs. Wilson thereupon requested the painting to be returned to the White House. There once more it hangs and tells its immortal lesson of how love can help life up the steepest hills.

Whilst in New York I visited the charming Fabians, who were the hosts of Maxim Gorky before the American Press took upon itself the rôle of doing the honours of the house to a guest of genius. The story of Gorky need not be repeated. But it is in itself a question-mark raised against the American civilisation.

———————

Tramping through Sandusky, I came upon a suburban house all scrawled over with chalk inscriptions :

" Hurrah for the newly-weds."

" Oh, you beautiful doll ! "

" Well !   *Then* what ? "

" We should worry."

" Home, sweet Home."

" May your troubles be little ones !   Ha, He ! "

" You thought we wouldn't guess, but we caught you."

As the house seemed to be empty, I inquired at the nearest store what was the reason for this outburst. The storekeeper told me it was done by the neighbours as a welcome to a newly-married couple coming home from their honeymoon on the morrow. It was a custom to do it, but this was nothing to the way they " tied them up " sometimes.

" Won't they be distressed ? "

" Oh no, they'll like it."

" Are the neighbours envious, or what is it ? " I asked. The storekeeper began to sing, " Snookey-ookums."

" All night long the neighbours shout

(to the newly-married couple whose kisses they hear)

" ' Cut it out, cut it out, cut it out.' "

———————

On Independence Day I saw a crowd of roughs assailing a Russian girl who had gone into the water to bathe, dressed in what we in Britain would call " full regulation costume." The crowd cried shame on her because she was not wearing stockings and a skirt in addition to knickers and vest.

———————

In many districts men bathing naked have been arrested as a sort of breach of the peace. Naked statues in public have been clothed or locked away. In several towns women wearing the slashed skirt have had to conform to municipal regulations concerning underwear.

———————

I have noted everywhere mockery on the heels of seri-ousness.

No doubt these question-marks will be followed by satis-factory answers in the minds of most readers, especially in the light of the statement that " it is a sacrament to walk the streets as an American citizen. Being an American is a sacred mission."

XIII.

ALONG ERIE SHORE.

CLEVELAND exemplifies the characteristics of contemporary America, and points to the future. It has its horde of foreign mercenaries living by alien ethics, and committing every now and then atrocious crimes which shock the American community. But it is a "cleaned-up" town. All the dens of the city have been raided; there is no gambling, little drunkenness and immorality. On my first night in the town I had my supper in a saloon, and as I sat among the beer-drinking couples I listened to an old man who was haranguing us all on the temptations of women and drink. The saloon-keeper had no power to turn him out, and possibly had not even the wish to do so. The passion for cleaning up America overtakes upon occasion even those whose living depends upon America remaining "unclean."

Cleveland is well built, and has fine avenues and broad streets. It is well kept, and in the drawing-room of the town you'd never suspect what was going on in the back kitchen and the yard. But take a turn about and you see that the city is not merely one of good clothes, white buildings, and upholstery; there are vistas of smoke and sun, bridges and cranes, endless railway tracks and steaming engines. They are working in the background, the Slavs and the Italians and the Hungarians, the Kikes and the Wops and the Hunkies. There is a rumour of Chicago in the air; you can feel the pulse of the hustling West.

Perhaps nothing is more promising than the twelve miles of garden suburb that go westward from the city along Erie Shore. Tchekof, working in his rose-garden in the Crimea, used to say, " I believe that in quite a short time the whole world will be a garden." This growth of Cleveland gives just that promise to the casual observer. How well these middle-class Americans live ! Without the advertisement of the fact, they have finer arrangements of streets and houses than we have at Golders Green and Letchworth. Nature is kind. There is a grand freshness and a steeping radiance. The people know how to live out-of-doors, and the women are public all day. No railings, fences, bushes, just sweet lawn approaches, verandahs, on the lawns sprinklers and automatic fountains scattering water to the sparrows' delight. The iris is out and the honeysuckle is in bloom.

I prefer, however, to walk in the sight of wooded hills or great waters, and as soon as I could find a way to the back of the long series of suburban villas I went to the sand-banks of the shore and into the company of the great lake. It was just sunset time, and the sun of fire was changing to a sun of blood and sinking into the waters. There was a great suffusion of crimson in the western sky and a reflection of it in the green and placid lake. But the water in the foreground was grey, and it rippled past silver reeds. I stood and listened ; the great silence of the vast lake on the one hand and the whiz of automobiles on the other, the *paup-paup* of electric-tram signals, the great whoop of the oncoming freight trains on the Lake-Shore railway. Far out on the water there were black dashes on the lit surface and little smokes proceeding from them—steamers. The lake became lucent yellow with blackness in the West and mystery in the East. A steamer in the East seemed fixed as if caught in a spell. Then the blackness of the West came like an intense dye and poured itself into the rest of the sky. The East became still—indigo, very precious and holy, the colour of incense smoke.

I tramped by Clifton through the deep dust of a motor-beaten road towards Lorain. It was night before I found a suitable place for sleeping, for most of the ground was private, and there were many people about. At last I found a deserted plot, where building operations had evidently been taking place during the day, but from which the workmen had gone. There were, however, many tools and covetable properties lying about, and I had hardly settled down before I heard the baying of dogs on a chain. About half-past eleven Fedka the watchman came along, singing a Russian song to himself, and he lighted a large lantern, unloosed two dogs, then went into a shed, lay down and went to sleep—a nice watchman! My only consideration was the dogs, a bull-dog and a collie, but they didn't know of my presence. They had expeditions after tramps on the road, after waggons, automobiles, tramcars, trains, but never once sniffed at the stranger sleeping under their noses. However, at about three in the morning the bull-dog spotted me, and no doubt had rather a queer turn. He actually tripped on me as he was prowling about, and my heart stood still. He eyed me, growled low, sniffed at my knees, snorted; " He will spring at my throat in a moment," I thought; " I'll defend myself with that big saw lying so handy beside me ! " But no, wonder of wonders ! the dog did not attack me, but just lay calmly down beside me and was my gaoler. He dozed and breathed heavily, but every now and then opened one eye and snarled ; evidently he took his duties seriously. I forgot him and slept. But I had the consciousness that in the morning I had to get away somehow.

But about half an hour before dawn some one drove a

score of cows down the road, causing the collie to go mad—
so mad that the bull-dog bestirred himself and followed
superciliously, not sure whether he were needed or not.
Then I swiftly put my things together and decamped—and
got away.

I watched the dawn come up out of a rosy mist over
Erie. The lake was vast and placid and mud-coloured,
but there were vague purple shadows in it. I learned that
mud was the real colour at this point, and there was no
clear sparkling water to bathe in, but only a sea stirred up.

Down by the shore, just after my dip, I caught a young
oriole with red breast and mouth so yellow, and I tried
to feed him with sugar and butter ; but he was very angry,
and from many trees and low bushes round about came the
scolding and calling of the parents, who had been rashly
giving their progeny his first run.

I tramped to the long settlement of Lorain with its
store-factory and many Polish workers, but continued to
the place called Vermilion, walking along the grey-black
sands of the shore. I came to Crystal Beach. It was a
perfect day, the zenith too radiant to look at, the western
sky ahead of the road a rising smoke of sapphire, but filled
with ineffable sunshine. It was difficult to look otherways
but downward, and I needed all the brim of my hat to
protect my neck and my eyes. The lake was now blue-
grey as the sea, but still not very tempting, though Crystal
Beach is a great holiday resort. It seemed to me more
than a lake and yet less than a sea—the water had no
other shore and yet suggested no infinity. The visitor,
however, considered it beautiful. That was clear from
the enthusiastic naming of the villas and resorts on the
shore. Again, it was strange to pass from the workshop
of America to the parlour,—from industrial Lorain to ease-
loving Vermilion, and to exchange the vision of unwashed

immigrants in slouch hats for dainty girls all in white and smart young men in delicate linen.

I went into the general store and bought butter and sugar and tea, and then to the baker for a loaf of bread and a peach pie. What a delicacy is an eightpenny peach pie when you know you are going to sit on a bank and munch it, drink coffee, and watch your own wood-blaze.

On my way to Sandusky I got several offers of jobs. A road surveyor and his man, trundling and springing along the road in their car, nearly ran me down, and as a compensation for my experience of danger stopped and gave me a lift, offering also to give me work if I wanted it. All the highway from Cleveland to Toledo was to be macadamised by next summer; thousands of men were wanted all along the line, and I could get to work that very afternoon " farming ditches on each side of the road " if I wished.

I jigged along three miles in the automobile and then stepped down to make my dinner. Whilst I was lighting my fire a Bohemian came and had a little chat with me.

" How far ye going ? "

" Chicago."

" You should get on a freight train. I come up from New York myself on a freighter and dropped off here two days ago. It's too far to walk ; you carry heavy things. Besides, there's a good job here mending the road. I've just been taken on. A mile up the road you'll see a waggon ; ask there, they're making up a gang. The work's a bit rough but the pay good."

Then I came on a gang of Wops and Huns loading bridge-props and ribbons and guard-rails on to an electric trolley, and the boss again applied to me.

" No, thanks ! "

A man with an asphalt and coal-oil scatterer came past. His was a dirty job. He sat behind a boiler-shaped cistern, which another man was dragging along with a petrol engine. It had a rose like a watering-cart, but instead of water there flowed this dark mixture of asphalt and oil. The man, a Lithuanian, was sitting on the rose, his legs were dangling under it, and it was his task to keep his finger on the tap and regulate the flow of the fast-trickling mixture. Though a Lithuanian by birth he spoke a fair English, and explained that the asphalt and oil laid the dust for the whole summer, and solidified the surface of the road, so that automobiles could go pleasantly along. There was another machine waiting behind, and they had not men to work it. If I liked to report myself at the depot I could get a job, it was quite simple, not hard work, and the pay was good. He got two dollars a day.

Then, as I was going through a little town, a Norwegian came running out of a shop and pulled me in, saying, "You're a professional, no doubt, stay here and take photographs"; and he showed me his screens and classical backgrounds. It was interesting to consider the many occasions on which I might have given up Europe and started as a young man in America, entering life afresh, and starting a new series of connections and acquaintances. But I had only come as a make-believe colonist.

As the weather was very hot I took a wayside seat erected by a firm of clothiers to advertise their wares, and it somewhat amused me to think that as I sat in my somewhat ragged and dust-stained attire that the seat seemed to say I bought my suit at Clayton's. As I sat there six Boy Scouts came tramping past, walking home from their camping-ground, boys of twelve or thirteen, all carrying saucepans and kettles, one of them a bag of medical appliances and medicines, all with heavy blankets —sun-browned, happy little bodies.

There is all manner of interest on the road. The gleam-

7

ing, red-headed woodpecker that I watch alights on the side of the telegraph-pole, looks at the wood as at a mirror, and then, to my mild surprise, goes right into the pole. There must be a hole there and a nest. I hear the guzzling of the little woodpeckers within. Upon reflection, I remember that the mother's beak was disparted, and there was something between. Rather amusing, a woodpecker living in a telegraph-pole—Nature taking advantage of civilisation!

Then there are many squirrels in the woods by the road, and they wag their tails when they squeak.

At tea-time, by the lake shore, a beautiful white-breasted but speckled snipe tripped around the sand, showing me his round head, plump body, and dainty legs. He had his worms and water, I my bread and tea; we were equals in a way.

Then after tea I caught a little blind mouse, no bigger than my thumb, held him in my hand, and put him in his probable hole.

As I rested by a railway arch Johnny Kishman, a fat German boy, got off his bicycle to find out what manner of man I was. His chief interest was to find out how much money I made by walking. And I flabbergasted him.

I came into Huron by a road of coal-dust, and left the beautiful country-side once more for another industrial inferno. Here were many cranes, black iron bridges, evil smells, an odorous green river. There was a continuous noise as of three rolls of thunder in one from the machinery of the port. I stopped a party of Slavs, who were strolling out of the town to the strains of an accordion, and asked them by what the noise was made. I was informed it was the lading of Pennsylvanian coal and the unlading of Wisconsin and Canadian ore, the tipping of five to ten tons at a time into the holds of coal boats or into trucks of freight trains.

I went into a restaurant in the dreary town, and there, over an ice-cream, chatted with an American, who hoped I would lick Jack London and Gibson and the rest of them " to a frazzle." A girl, who came into the shop, told me that last year she wanted to walk to Chicago and sleep out, but could not get a companion—a chance for me to step in. Mine host was one of these waggish commercial men in whom America abounds, and he had posted above his bar :

ELEVEN MEN WHO ASKED
CREDIT
LIE DEAD IN MY CELLAR.

But he made good ice-cream.

Every one combined to boost the town and advise me to see this and that. The port machinery and lading operations were the wonder of Erie Shore, and provided work for a great number of Hungarians, Italians, and Slavs. Not so many years back there was no such machinery here, and the work was done with buckets and derricks.

I forbore to have supper at the creditless inn, but as I walked out of the dark town I spied a fire burning on a bit of waste land, and there I boiled my kettle and made coffee. It was an eerie proceeding, and as I sat in the dusk I saw several children come peering at me, *hsh*ing the younger ones, and inferring horrible suspicions as to my identity. When I had finished my supper I went down to the beach, and there, on the sand amidst old logs, under a stooping willow tree, I made my bed.

It was a wonderful, placid night after a long, hot day. The smoke-coloured lake was weakly plashing. There was no sign of the past sunset in the west, and smoke seemed to be rising from the darkness of the horizon. The one light on the city pier had its stab of reflection in the water below. Near me, still trees leant over the water. The branches and leaves of the willow under which I slept were delicately figured against the sky as I looked upward, and far away over the lake the faint stars glimmered. The moon stood high in the south, and illumined the surface of the waters and the long coast line of the bay.

When I awoke next morning, what a sight! The blue-grey lake so placid, just breathing, that's all, and crimson ripples stealing over it from the illuminated smoky east. It was clear that the smokiness of the horizon came from real smoke—from all the chimneys and stacks of Huron. I saw massed volumes of it hurrying away from the docks and the works, and standing out on the lake like a great wall. As I lay on my spread on the sand, looking out idly with my cheek on my hand, I saw the sun come sailing through the smoke like a red balloon. No celestial sunrise this, but Nature beautifully thwarted.

I made a fire and cooked my breakfast, and sat on a log enjoying it; and all the while the sun strove to be himself and shine in splendour over the new world, whose beauties he himself had called into being. For a whole hour, though there was not a cloud in the sky or a mist on the lake, he made no more progress than on a foggy January morning in London. He gave no warmth to speak of; he was an immaterial, luminous moon.

But at last he got free, and began to rise indeed, exchanging the ragged crimson reflection in the water for a broad-bladed flashing silver dagger. A great glory grew about him; all the wavelets of the far lake knew him and looked up to him with their tiny faces. His messengers searched the horizon for the shadows of night, for all lingering wraiths and mists, and banished them. The smoky door by which the sun had come out of the east was shut after him. But he shed so much light that you could not see the door any longer.

I went in for a swim, and as I was playing about in the sunlit water the first human messenger of the morning came past me—a fisherman in a tooting, panting motor-boat, dragging fishing-nets after him. He gave me greeting in the water.

Fishing is good here—as a trade. Every day many tons of carp are unloaded. The fish are caught in gill-nets—nets with a mesh from which the fishes are unable to extricate themselves, their gills getting caught. The nets are framed on stakes, floated by corks and steadied by leads. The fishermen leave them standing two or three days, and when the fish are wearied out or dead they haul them in.

This very hot day I marched to an accompaniment of the thunder of the dock-works, and reached Sandusky, —a very large industrial port, the junction of three railways, not a place of much wealth, its population at least half foreign.

I had a shave at a negro barber's, and chatted with the darkie as he brandished the razor.

After the war he and his folks had come north and settled in Michigan. He sent all his children to college. One was earning a hundred and twenty-five dollars a month as music-mistress in Washington.

" They treat you better up here than in the South ? " said I.

" Why, yes ! "

" And in London better still."

" Oh, I know. My father went to London. He stayed at a big hotel, and there turned up three Southerners. They went up to the hotel-keeper and said, ' Look hyar, that coloured feller 'll have to go ; we cahn stay here with him ! ' And the hotel-keeper said, ' If he don't please you, *you* go ; we won't keep you back.' "

" Very affecting," said I.

" There was a fellah came hyar to play the organ for the Episcopal Church," the negro went on. " He was called Street. The other fellah was only fit to turn the music for him. He had the goods, b'God he had. Tha's what I told them."

With that I got away. Outside the shop a hawker cried out to me :

" Kahm'ere ! "

" What d'you want ? " said I.

" I've a good safety razor."

" Don't use them."

" A fountain pen to write home to your wife. . . . "

The hawker had many wares.

I spent the night in a saloon at Venice, and watched the rate at which German fishermen can drink beer.

Next morning I walked across Sandusky Bay by the Lake Shore railway-bridge, a mile and a half long—an unpleasant business, watching for the express trains and avoiding being run over. At last I got to Danbury, and could escape from the rails to the cinder-path at the side. The engine-drivers and firemen of the freight trains greeted me as they passed me, and now and then I was able to offer " Casey Jones " a cup of coffee and exchange gossip.

The enormous freight trains told their tale of the internal trade of America ; on no other lines of railway in the world could you witness such processions of produce. All sorts of things flew past on these lumberous trains—cars full of hogs with hundreds of motionless black snouts poking between the bars ; refrigerator cars full of ham—dead hogs, dripping and slopping water as they went along in the heat, and the sun melted the ice ; cars of coal ; open

cars of bright glistening tin-scraps going to be molten a
second time; cars of agricultural machinery; cars laden
with gangs of immigrant men being taken to work on a
big job by labour contractors; closed cars full of all manner
of unrevealed merchandise and machinery. On the cars,
the names of the railways of America—Illinois Central,
Wabash, Big Four, Lake Shore. . . .

At Gypsum I returned to the high road, and there
once more had an offer of a job from a gang. I was surprised to see boys of thirteen or fourteen hard at work with
spade and shovel.

" I see you're working for your living," said I.

" What's the matter with you ? "

" I said ' You're working for your living.' "

" Wahn a jahb ? "

" No; I'm not looking for one. I'm walking to Chicago."

A contractor came forward, a short Frenchman in
waistcoat and shirt-sleeves. His bowler hat was pushed
to the back of his head, and his hair poked out from under
it over his scarred, perspiring brow. He was not working
—only directing.

" What would *you* be ? A sort of tramp ? " said he.
" I used to have a hobo-station at Toledo. I've seen the
shiner * line up sixty or seventy of them and send them
to work with car fare paid. They'd work half a day and
then disappear mysteriously. We have pay-day once in
two weeks; but these tramps, many of them educated
fellers too, would never work the time through or wait
for their pay. Thousands of dollars have been lost by
hoboes who gave up their jobs before pay-day."

There was an Englishman from Northampton in the
gang, and he testified that America had " England licked
ten times over."

* Policeman.

There were fat Germans in blouses, mustachioed Italians with black felt hats pulled down over sunburnt, furrowed brows. All the men and the boys were suffering from a sort of " tar blaze " in the face. They were glad to ease up a little to talk to me ; but they had a watchful eye on the face of the boss, who besides being contractor was a sort of timekeeper.

The contractor was vexed that I wouldn't take a job. Labour was scarce. He averred that before I reached Chicago the farmers would come on to the road and compel me to work on their fields. Trains had been held up before now.

" I thought slavery was abolished ? " said I.

The next town on my route was Port Clinton, a bright little city, and in the eyes of at least one of its citizens a very important one. I had a long talk with a chance-met journalist and the keeper of a fruit-shop. The journalist, by way of interviewing me, told me all I wanted to know about the district. Fruit-growing was far in advance here. Perry Camp, the greatest shooting-butts in the world, was near by. The Lake Shore railway was going to spend a million dollars in order to shorten the track a quarter of a mile. The greengrocer told me I had the face of a Scotsman, but spoke English like a Swede—which just shows how badly Americans speak our tongue, and hear it as a rule.

In the course of my interview I confessed that for roadside literature I read the Gospel of St. John and the Book of Revelation, a chapter a day, and when I came to the end of either book I started again. The greengrocer interrupted the journalist, and said :

" When you're tired, you just take out the Bible and read a little, eh, and you get strength and go on ? I knew you were that sort when I saw you first coming up the other side of the road, and I said to my friend, ' He reads his Bible.' "

The greengrocer was much edified, and told me that he was the agent for the district of Billy Sunday, the revivalist. Wouldn't I stay and address a mass meeting?

I fought shy of this offer. The journalist looked somewhat sourly at the greengrocer for breaking into his interrogatory. But then a third interrupter appeared, a little boy, who had come to purchase bananas, and he addressed me thus:

" On which side did your family fight in the year 1745? On the side of Prince Charlie? That's the side I'm on."

No descendant of the Pilgrim Fathers he.

On the way out to Lacarne two old fishermen in a cart offered me a ride, and I stepped up.

" What are you, German? " I asked, always on the look-out for the immigrant.

" We are Yankees."

" Your father or grandfather came from Germany? "

" No; we're both Yankees, I tell yer."

" I suppose your ancestors came from England then."

" No; we've always bin 'ere."

They had been out three nights seine-fishing on the lake, were very tired, and rewarded themselves with swigs of rum every now and then, passing the bottle from one to the other and then to me with real but suspicious hospitality. Their families had always been in America. The fact that they came originally from England meant no more to them than Hengist and Horsa does to some of us.

By the way, Hengist and Horsa were a couple of savages, were they not?

The fishermen put me down beside a plantation, which they said was just the place in which to sleep the night.

7 a

I wasn't sorry to get on to my feet again, and I watched them out of sight,—fat, old, sleepy, hospitable ruffians.

The plantation was a mosquito-infested swamp, and I did not take the fishermen's advice. Myriads of "husky" mosquitoes were in the air, the unpleasanter sort, with feathered antennæ, and whenever I stood still on the road scores of "Canadian soldiers" settled on me, a loathsome but innocuous species of diptera.

I sought shelter of man that night, and through the hospitality of a Slav workman found a place in a freight train —a strange bed that not only allows you to sleep, but takes you a dozen miles farther on in the morning. The engine-driver told me that there was a "whole bunch of tramps" on the train, but that no one ever turned tramps off an empty freight train,—not on the Lake Shore railway at any rate.

When I "dropped" from the freighter I found myself at Elliston, and commenced there a day of delicious tramping. The opal dawn gave birth to a great white horse of cloud, and out of the cloud came a strong fresh breeze, having health and happiness on its wings. A quiet Sunday. I reached Toledo this day—and parted company with Erie Shore—great, busy, happy, prosperous Toledo. It was strange to exchange the country for the town; to come out of the green, fresh, silent landscape into the close, stifling, bustling town, full of promenaders talking and laughing among themselves vociferously.

As I came into the city the day-excursion boat was just about to start on the return journey to Detroit. Excursionists were flocking together to the quay, a great spectacle to a Briton. All the men were carrying their coats in their arms, many had their collars off and the neckbands of their shirts turned down, bunches of carnations on their naked chests; many were without waistcoats, and had tickets with the name of their town pinned to their fancy-coloured shirts; the red, perspiring, glistening faces of many of them suggested an over-confidence in beer as a quencher of thirst. The women carried parasols of coloured paper. They were all in white, and were so thinly clad that you asked yourself why they were so thin. But despite all precautions the sun had marked everybody, but marked them kindly.

Suddenly a bell was rung on the steamer, and a little man came forward and announced in broken English:

"Somebody wan' to come on the boat; the time is supp."

XIV.

THE AMERICAN LANGUAGE.

EVEN Americans of the highest culture and of Boston families speak English differently from any people in the old country. The difference may not be obvious to all, but it is there, and it is a thing to rejoice in, not to be sorry for. The American nation is different from the British, has different history and a different hope ; it has a different soul, therefore its expression should be different. The American face as a type is different ; it would be folly to correct the words of the mouth by Oxford, or Eton, or Granville Barker's theatre, or the cultured Aberdonian, or any other criterion. The use of American expressions of quite moderate tone amounts to a breach of good taste in many British drawing-rooms ; and if you tell a story in which American conversation is repeated with the accent imitated, you can feel the temperature going down as you proceed ; that is, if you are not merely making fun of the Americans. Making fun of any foreign people is always tolerable to the British ; a truly national and insular trait. The literary world and the working men and women of Britain can enter into the American spirit, and even imitate it upon occasion ; but that is only the misfortune of our populace, who ought to be finding national expression in journalism and music-hall songs and dancing, and who are merely going off the lines by imitating a foreign country. It is loss to Britain that the Americans speak a comprehensible dialect of our tongue, and that the journalist of Fleet Street, when he is hard-up for wit, should take scissors and paste and snip out stories from American papers; or that commercial *entrepreneurs* should bring to the British public things thought to be sure of success because they have succeeded in America—" Within the Law," " I Should Worry," " Hullo Ragtime ! " and the rest. The people who are surest in instinct, though they are sympathetic to a brother-people, hate the importation of foreign uglinesses, and the substitution of foreign for local talent.

The American language is chiefly distinguished from the British by its emphatic expressive character. Britain, as I have said, lives in a tradition ; America in a passion. We are laconic, accidental, inarticulate ; our duty is plain, and we do it without words. But the American is affirmative, emphatic, striving ; he has to find out what he's going to do next, and he has got to use strong words. Britain also is the place of an acknowledged Caste system ; but America is the place of equal citizens, and many American expressions are watchdogs of freedom and instruments of mockery, which reduce to a common dimension any people who may give themselves airs.

The subtler difference is that of rhythm. American blood flows in a different *tempo*, and her hopes keep different measure.

.   .   .   .   .   .

Americans commonly tell us that theirs is the language of Shakespeare and Shakespearian England, and that they have in America the " well of English undefiled." But if they have any purely European English in that country it must be a curiosity. Shakespeare was a lingual junction, but we've both gone on a long way since then, and in our triangle the line subtending the Shakespearian angle gets longer and longer. O. Henry makes a character in one of his stories write a telegram in American phraseology, so that it shall be quite unintelligible to people who only know English :

His nibs skedaddled yesterday per jack-rabbit line with all the coin in the kitty and the bundle of muslin he's spoony about. The boodle is six figures short. Our crowd in good shape, but we need the spondulicks. You collar it. The main guy and the dry goods are headed for the briny. You know what to do.—BOB.

This is not Shakespearian English, but of course it is not Shakespearian American. The worst of the contemporary language of America is that it is in the act of changing its skin. It is difficult to say what is permanent and what is merely eruptive and dropping. Such expressions as those italicised in the following examples are hardly permanent :

" One, two, three, *cut it out* and work for Socialism."

" *I should worry* and get thin as a lamp-post so that tramps should come and lean against me."

" *Him with the polished dome.*"

" She hadn't been here two days before I saw her kissing the boss. Well, said I, *that's going some.*"

" This is Number Nine of the Ibsen *highbrow* series."

" *Do you get me ?* "

" I'll *put you wise.*"

" And how is your *yoke-mate ?* "

" He thinks too much of himself : *too much breathed on by girls.*"

" A low lot of *wops and hunkies : white trash.*"

" Poor negroes ; *coloured trash.*"

" She is *one good-looker.*"

" She is *one sweetie.*"

" My ! You have *a flossy hat.*"

But I suppose " He is a white man " is permanent, and " Buy a postcard, it'll *only set you back a nickel.*"

" She began to lay down the law : *thus and so.*"

" Now *beat it !* "

" Roosevelt went ranching, that's how he got so *husky*."

" Is it far ?   It is only *a little ways*."

" Did they *feed that to you* ? "

" When he started he was in a poor way, and carried in his hay in his arms, but now he is quite *healed*."

But the difference in speech is too widespread and too subtle to be truly indicated by this collection of examples, and the real vital growth of the language is independent of the flaming reds and yellows of falling leaves. In the course of conversation with Americans you hear plenty of turns of expression that are unfamiliar, and that are not merely the originality of the person talking. Thus in :

" How do they get on now they are married ? "

" Oh, she has him feeding out of her hand,"

though the answer is clear it owes its form to the American atmosphere.

Or again in :

" I suppose she's sad now he's gone ? "

" Oh ! He wasn't a pile of beans to her, believe me,"

you feel the manner of speech belongs to the new American language. The following parody of President Wilson's way of speaking is also an example of the atmosphere of the American language :

So far as the prognosticationary and symptomatic problemaciousness of your inquiry is concerned it appears to me that while the trusts should be regulated with the most unrelentful and absquatulatory rigorosity, yet on the other hand their feelings should not be lacerated by rambunktions and obfusticationary harshness.   Do you bite that off ?

Punch would have no stomach for such Rabelaisian vigour.

But wherever you go, not only in the cities, but in the little towns, you hear things never heard in Britain. I go into a country bakery, and whilst I ask for bread at one counter I hear behind me at the other :

" Kendy, ma-ma, kendy ! "

" Cut it out, Kenneth."

" Kendy, kendy, kendy ! "

" Oh, Kenneth, cut it out ! "

Or, as I sit on a bank, a girl of twelve and her little baby sister come toddling up the road. The little one loses her slipper, and the elder cries out :

" Slipper off again !   Ethel, perish ! "

America must necessarily develop away from us at an ever-increasing rate. Influenced as she is by Jews, Negroes, Germans, Slavs, more and more foreign constructions will creep into the language,—such things as " I should worry," derived from Russian-Jewish girl strikers. " She ast me for a nickel," said a Jew-girl to me of a passing beggar. " *I should give her a nickel*, let her work for it same as other people ! " The *I shoulds* of the Jew can pass into the language of the Americans, and be understood from New York to San Francisco ; but such expressions make no progress in Great Britain, though brought over there, just because we have not the big Jewish factor that the Americans have.

To-day the influence that has come to most fruition is that of the negro. The negro's way of speaking has become the way of most ordinary Americans, but that influence is passing, and in ten or twenty years the Americans will be speaking very differently from what they are now. The foreigner will have modified much of the language and many of the rhythms of speech. America will have less self-consciousness then. She will not be exploiting the immigrant, but will be subject to a very powerful influence from the immigrants. No one will then be so cheap as the poor immigrant is to-day. Much mean nomenclature will have disappeared from the language, many cheap expressions, much mockery; on the other hand, there will be a great gain in dignity, in richness, in tenderness.

XV.

THROUGH THE HEART OF THE COUNTRY.

I HAVE come to that portion of my journeying and of my story where all day, every evening, and all night long I was conscious of the odour of mown clover, of fields of ambrosia.

I was tramping along the border of Northern Ohio and Southern Michigan, from Toledo to Angola, Indiana. I was entering the rich West. The fields were vast and square, the road was long and flat, and straight and quiet, the June haze hung over luxuriant meadows, and there was a wonderful silence and ripening peace over the country.

One evening, as the red sun sank into night-darkened mist, I talked with an old farmer, who was smoking his pipe at his gate.

"I came along this same road like you, with a bundle on my back, forty years ago," said he, "and I took work on a farm; then I rented a farm. Many's the lad I've seen go past of an evening. And one or two have stopped here and worked some days, for the matter of that."

The farmer had left England when he was a stripling, and I tried to talk to him of the old country, but he was not really interested. He did not want to go back.

That is the Colonial feeling.

Strange to plough all day, or sow or reap, and in the evening to return to the quiet, solitary house of wood beside the great red-painted barn and not want England or Europe, not be interested in it, not want anything more than you've got; to have the sun go down red and whisper nought, and the stars come up and the moon, and yet not yearn; to work, to eat, to market; to have children growing about you ripening in so many years, and corn springing up in the fields ripening in so many weeks; births, marriages, deaths, sowings, harvests. . . .

There is all the pathos of man's life in it.

I slept that night in the dry wayside hay, under the broad sky and the misty golden moon. It was a quiet night, warm and gentle. Earth held the wanderer in her cradle and rocked him to sleep.

They are kind people about here. Next morning as I sat by my fire a woman sent her son out to me with a quart of milk and a bag of cookies. And milk is a much commercialised business on this western road,—the electric freight train carries nearly all the milk away in churns to Toledo. It was a very welcome talkative boy who brought out the milk. His father rented one-third of a section (213 acres), but was now laid up with pneumonia. As a consequence of the father's illness the young children had to work very hard in the fields. And there was a sick cow on the farm—sick through eating rank clover. And the boy himself had had scarlet fever in the spring. The serving-girl had had to go away " to have her little baby," and the one that came in her place brought the fever.

" What's your name ? " said I.

" Charles."

Cheerful little Charles. He had much responsibility on his shoulders.

There were some big farms along the road, and near Metamora I had the privilege of seeing a dozen cows milked simultaneously by a petrol engine, rubber tubes being fixed to their teats and the milk pumped out. It was astonishing, the matter-of-fact way in which the latest invention was applied to farm life.

" It's rather ugly," said I.

" Well, what are you to do when labour is so scarce ? " was the reply.

Land is rich here, but labour is scarce. I fell in with a garrulous farmer who told me that land now sold at 150 dollars (£30) the acre, and that in a few years it would rise to 250 dollars. The days of large farmers were over. All the big ranches were being sold up, and the farmers were taking holdings that they could farm themselves without help. Labour was expensive, owing to the high wages paid in the towns for industrial work ; even at two and a half dollars (ten shillings) a day it was difficult to get a decent gang to do the work in the harvest season. You could do better with a small piece of land. Fields here were forty and fifty acres, and the steam plough was not used. In the old days land was dirt cheap, and you could buy vast tracts of it ; there were no taxes, no extra expenses, and you just went in to raise tremendous crops and make a big scoop. To-day things were different. To work on a large scale a horde of labourers was necessary. But now the Socialists were stopping the flow of immigrants into the country. Socialists said that it was too difficult to organise newcomers. The newcomers behaved like blacklegs, strike-breakers, all the first year of their stay in America. They didn't know the language, were very poor, suspected their brother workmen of jealousy, and just took any wage offered them. The Socialists wanted to keep the price of labour up, and my farmer friend bore them a grudge because it was difficult to develop the land unless the price was reduced.

A little later, outside Fred M'Gurer's farm, the jovial farmer himself came and squatted beside the fire and chatted of affairs. He had insured his house for 1000 dollars, but it would take 1800 dollars to rebuild it. "I think it's only fair to take some of the risk myself," said he ; "and if the place burns down the company will know I didn't set it alight o' purpose."

Fifty-eight years old is Fred M'Gurer, and his son is now coming to live and work with him altogether, after seven years spent wintering in the city and summering in the country. Irish once, and of an Irish family—but they go to no church. The old man feels that he is a Christian all the same, and will get to heaven at last, because he "deals square with his fellow-men."

Fred and his son work the farm all by themselves, outside labour is so expensive. The beet-fields take all the immigrants. Did I see the red waggons as I came along, full of Flemish and Russians living by beet-picking on the beetroot farms near by ?

I saw them.

"America is a high hill for them that don't speak the language," said Fred. But he said that because he likes talking himself, and can't imagine himself in a land where he could not hold converse. The immigrants manage very well without the language, and scale the hill, and rake in the dollars easily. Perhaps they do not glean much of the American ideal, and the hope of the American nation. But I suppose Fred did not mean that.

I had a pleasant talk with a successful German farmer, who took me in a cart from Pioneer to Grizier, through comparatively poor country. He had possessed a farm of five acres in Germany, but there each acre had been worth between 450 and 500 dollars. When he came to Grizier land was selling at 25 dollars an acre, and he was able to buy fifty acres of it and to bring up his family in health and plenty. His farm was now worth more than 5000 dollars.

I slept on an old waggon in a wheat-field near Grizier ; but about midnight it began to rain, and I was obliged to seek shelter in a crazy, doorless, windowless cottage, and there I sat all the next day and slept all the next night whilst the elements raged. In the cottage were two chairs, a home-made table, and a broken bedstead. I cooked my meals on the rainy threshold. The refuge was shared by a great big bumble-bee, two red-admirals, a brown squirrel, and two robins.

The second morning was Sunday, radiant, fresh, and green. The road was soft but clean, with yielding cakes of mud ; the grass was fresh, for every blade had been washed on Saturday ; the wild strawberry was a brighter ruby ; on spread bushes the wild rose was in bloom ; there were sun-browned country girls upon the road, who were shy but might be spoken to ; the odour of clover was purer, the hay-fields had round shoulders after the storm, and you'd think cows had been lying down where the wind had laid the tussocks low. The sun shone as if it had forgotten it had shone before, and was doing it for the first time. To-day it became evident that the grain was ripening ; the apple trees in fantastic shapes were knee-deep in yellowing corn. The little oak trees by the side of the road presented foliage, every leaf of which looked as if it had been carefully polished.

In America wild strawberries are three on a stalk, which causes a pleasant profusion. . . .

I got a whole loaf of home-made bread given me at Cooney . . ., and a quart of milk at " Fertile Valley Farm." . . .

Only at sunset did I strike the main Angola Road, and off that road I made my bed in a wheat-field and fell asleep, watching the bearded ears disproportionately magnified and black in the flame of the crimson sky. Next day, when I awoke, life was just creeping into the blue-green night, a soft radiance as of rose petals was in the east, and a breeze was wandering like a rat among the stalks of the wheat. I fell asleep again, and when I reopened my eyes it was bright morning.

The Sunday gave way to the week-day. There is nothing happening on the roads on the Sunday; the tramp is left with Nature, but directly Monday comes the work and life of the people reveal themselves, and adventures are more frequent.

My first visitor this Monday was a man of business. As I was making my tea he came up towards me driving two lean horses and a great black oblong box on wheels. At the farm where I had drawn water for my kettle he pulled up and dismounted. A girl who had seen him from a window of the farm-house came tripping to meet him. He exchanged some words with her, and then from the far side of his hearse-like cart he produced a black chest, out of which he pulled a pair of boots. The young lady then hopped back to the house to try them on. Satisfied as to her purchase, she took in addition a pound of tea and a packet of sugar. The cart was a moving store : here were all manner of things for sale. But the storekeeper received no money; all his debts were paid in eggs. One side of the hearse was full of merchandise, the other contained nested boxes and crates for the accommodation of hundreds of dozens of eggs.

The storeman gave me a lift and explained to me his business. He possessed a cold-storage establishment in the city; he credited the farm people with sixteen cents (eight-pence) for every dozen eggs they gave him, then he stored them in his freezing-house till autumn, when they could be thrown on the market at twenty-five to thirty cents the dozen.

He was a great believer in cold storage. "Meat," said he, "is tenderer when it has been frozen some weeks."

Business in eggs used to be better. Now the State set a limit on the time you could keep them in cold storage. Sometimes he had to sell out at a loss. The hope was to keep all the farm produce till there was a real scarcity and prices went high. Then it would be possible to make a small fortune.

"But I'm tired of this business," said the storeman; "I'd like to give it up and buy land."

We lumbered along the road and stopped at each farmhouse. Sometimes we sold articles, but whether we sold anything or not we always took a few dozen eggs; every farmer was in business with my man and used him as a sort of egg-bank. Even if they were not in debt to him they were glad to hand over their eggs and be credited with the corresponding amount of money. We took four or five dozen eggs at least at every farm, and sometimes as many as twenty and thirty dozen. The storeman left behind an empty crate at each farm, so that it might be filled for him next time he came along, and he took aboard the crate already filled. In exchange he sold kerchiefs, boots, corsets, cloth, brooms, brushes, coffee, corn-flake, wire-gauze to keep out mosquitoes, etc. At the end of his round he would have got rid of almost all his merchandise and have filled both sides of the hearse with eggs. He took home upon occasion as many as five hundred dozen eggs!

A cheerful American with a word of news, a titbit of gossip, and the top of the morning for all the country women. He was eagerly awaited, and children at farmgates descried him a long way off and ran in to tell their mothers. Even the babies were excited at his approach, for they knew he carried a supply of candy. At each farm where there was a baby the storeman left a little bag of candy. He knew the value of good-will.

" It's a good business," said he ; " no expense of keeping a shop, double profit,—profit on the goods and profit on the eggs ; it pays all right. But I'm tired of it, and I think I shall give it up and buy land." To several of his customers who asked after his business he replied in the same terms. He was getting tired of it, and was thinking of buying land. When I took a photograph of his cart and himself he said he would be very glad to have a copy, just to remind him of old days—for he was thinking of giving it up, etc.

It is interesting to observe the commercialisation that goes on in the country in America. Not only does the egg-bank and travelling store come round, but the cream-vans come also and buy up all the cream, and the baker comes from the bread factory and dumps, twice or three times a week, huge baskets of damp, tasteless loaves, all wrapped in grease-paper. Not many people bake their own bread—they save time and take this astonishing substitute. Then travellers in coffee have exploited special brands—" Euclid Coffee," " Primus Coffee," " Old Reliable," and the like, done up in pound packets. Rural Americans do not realise that good coffee is coffee and no more.

No one had a quart of milk to spare on the road to Angola, so I hit on a plan which I recommend to others in like circumstances. I went to a farm-house and asked for a cupful of milk to have with my coffee ; I got it easily and freely. The farmer was rather touched. But as you cannot make decent coffee with one cupful of milk I went to another farm and begged another cupful, and then to another. I was able to make a good pot of coffee, despite the scarcity of milk.

Whilst I was having lunch, I had an interesting talk

with an ancient man who was mowing grass at the side of the road.

" You look like Father Time," said I.

" Well, I've mown a good many days," he replied. " I shall soon die now. There's no strength in me ; my day is over."

" Have you enjoyed life ? " I asked.

" Yes, I have," he replied, his face lighting up.

" Do you work your farm yourself ? "

" No ! My son works it ; he is twenty-two. Yes, I married late. Thirty-two years I wandered as you are doing. I've been in thirty states. I was ten years on the Lakes, a sailor."

" Ever across the Atlantic ? "

" Never on the big waters."

" And how do you think America is going on ? "

" I think she is going bad. The new generation is weak. There'll soon be no old farmer stock. The old folk work, but the children go to school. My father was an old Connecticut Yankee—a republican—so am I ; but the party has broken up, the country's going wild."

The old man had a dog " Colonel," named after Colonel Somebody, who was his father's Squire in Connecticut.

" A fine dog," said I.

" More helpful than a boy," said the old farmer. " He can drive the hog home straight, and he always helps me up when I tumble down I'm weak now—have had two strokes, and after the last I was just like a baby. I can't mow properly—no strength to move anything. Often I fall of a heap, and Colonel runs in and gets under my stomach with his head and raises me. A 'cute dog. . . ."

A pleasant vision of not unhappy age !

I passed through Angola—a neat little city round about a shoppy square ; a quiet market-place functionising the agricultural country round about. I had dinner at one of several restaurants, and had three quick-lunch courses brought to me at once—an array of nine or ten plates on a little grey stone table—not very appetising.

There were three or four country loungers at the ice-cream bar of the establishment, and a negro was sitting at another table with a tall glass and a straw and a " soda." At my side was what I took to be a piano—very dusty, and with the keyboard out of sight. Suddenly, without any warning, it jumped into music, and thumped out a cake-walk in its interior. It was as if a lot of niggers were doing the dance in an empty room.

I paid no attention, facially. Alas ! we are quite familiar with such marvels, with all that can be shown. We raise no eyebrow. But bring in an aboriginal Chinee and sit him there where I was, and start this box a-going, and he'd jump out of his wits. How was it started ? Some one went softly across the room and put a cent in a slot—that's all. Is it not maddening to be uninterested, unthrilled ? None of us paid any attention. The loungers gossiped with the ice-cream girl, the nigger drew up his soda, I strove with my hard roast beef.

. . . . . .

St. John's Eve ! Unusual things might be expected to happen this night. I had lived with the growing summer, had caught in my hands one evening not long since a large dusky lovely emperor-moth, and had received an invitation from fairyland. The strange thing was that as I tramped out of Angola on the Lagrange Road, it did not occur. to me what day it was. Only in the middle of the night did I reflect—there is something unusual astir, something is happening all about me, this is no ordinary night. And only in the morning did I realise it had been St. John's Eve.

I slept by an orchard on a hill. Below me was a little

lake, on the right a straw stack, on the left an apple tree, over me a plum tree with wee plums. All night long little apples fell from their weak stalks, the frogs sang—now solos, now choruses, the mosquitoes hummed in the plum tree. On the surface of the little lake little lights appeared and disappeared as the wandering fireflies carried messages from reed to reed. Processions of clouds stole over the starry sky, and I thought of rain, but the whole night was hot and odorous and full of dreams.

I did not awake next morning till it was bright day. Between me and the straw stack there was a fluttering and squawking of young birds being taught to fly by their mother. Every time a young bird alighted after a little flutter, it always fell on its nose. My attention was divided between the birds and a big bee, who thought I had made my bed over his nest. What a distressing way the bumble-bee has of losing himself and thinking you are to blame!

I tramped to the reedy lake of Whip-poor-Will. The wind blew now hot from the sun's mouth, now cold from a cloud's shoulder. The question was, Would the Midsummer day turn to heat or come to rain? It turned to heat. What a day of happiness I spent on the sandy ups and downs of country roads! After weeks among plains, I was glad of a country-side that had corners again. I was among " dear little lakes," the children of the great lakes— in the nursery.

I came to Flint, and met the " pike road " from Detroit to Chicago. Flint has a large general store and a barber's shop. I bought three oranges out of the refrigerator of the store, and, to make them last longer, half a pound of honey-cakes.

At noon I made my midday fire in the bed of a dried-up rivulet. The weather was almost too hot for tending a fire ; tawny spots appeared on my wrists, and, viewing my face in the metal back of my soap-box, I was startled to see the fire in my eyebrows and cheeks. But with the heat there was a wind, and in the afternoon great cumuli grew up in the sky, and it was possible to think the earth was a ship and the clouds the billows which we were rolling over. Up hill and down dale, round corners, by snug farms with green and crimson cherry orchards, over hills where miles of corn were blanching and waving! I came to Brushy Prairie, and camped for the night in an angle of the road beside the village cemetery.

I read and wrote, mended my clothes, cleaned my pack of waste dust, collected hay to make a bed. Many carts came past, and the people in them hailed me with facetious remarks. After I had lain down one old village wife came to see if I were sick and wanted medicine. It was strange to lie by the cemetery and hear a party of girls go by in a buggy, singing, " When the roll is called up yonder, I'll be there."

I lay and watched the sky, scanning the clouds for a certitude of a dry night. A great war was going on between the forces of the clear sky and of the clouds. There was a party of skirmishers advancing from the south-west. There was a long array of clouds in the north and in the south, and the main army lay heavy and invincible in the north-west. But the clear sky scattered the enemy wherever it encountered them, and even forced the main army to take up a new position. The camp of the clouds was made far away, and lights came out in their leaguer.

The night became silent and brilliant and perfect, and I lay with my eyes open, and did not look, but just saw. . . .

I slept. Whilst my eyes were closed there was a great night attack, and when I woke again I found the armies of the clear sky completely routed. There was a shower of rain, and I jumped up and tripped along to the church.

The door was open. I struck a match and saw all the pews and prayer-books and hymn-sheets, and away in the shadows the platform and the pulpit.

But the shower ceased. I reflected that if heavy rain came on I could easily come into shelter, so I returned to my hay-spread, and lay down again and watched the renewed battle in the sky.

A desperate rally! One star, two stars were shining, and round about them a great stand was being made. They fought lustily. They seemed to be gaining ground. Yes. Three, four, five stars showed, six. . . . I fell asleep again, knowing that the side I favoured would win. When I wakened next it was to greet the great General coming from the East in all his war-paint, and hung all over with silver medals. A glorious day followed.

I spent a morning by the clear St. Joseph River. On the road to Middlebury wild raspberries abounded. I could have picked a pound or so of berries along the road. Raspberry bushes occur in many places, but I've seen few raspberries hitherto. That is because the great friends of the raspberries live so near—human boys and girls—and they are always taking the raspberries to school, to church, to the corn-field. If they are going home they insist on taking the little raspberries home too, to the distress of fathers and mothers sometimes, for the raspberries know how to disagree with the children upon occasion, especially the young ones.

There were not many farm-houses about here, but at one of them I was given a pot full of ripe cherries, and made a " smash " of them, and ate them with milk and sugar.

A motorist took me along a dozen miles in a bouncing, petrol-spurting runabout car, a Dutchman, who paid me the compliment of saying I spoke very grammatically for a foreigner.

There was a thundershower in the afternoon. In the evening I obtained permission to sleep in a barn, and the farmer talked to me as I lay in the straw. There had been a runaway team the day before, and his neighbour's bay mare had twenty-four stitches in her now, and he didn't reckon she'd be much more good.

A waggoner taking fowls and dairy produce to sell at restaurants and quick-lunch shops took me into Elkhart next morning. Elkhart is a large city, with many car factories and buggy factories, and by comparison with the country round is very foreign, full of Italians, Poles, and Jews. It is a well-built, handsome city, with much promise for the future.

As I stepped out on the Shipshewaka Road I saw by a notice that a prize was being offered for the most popular woman and the homeliest man. What a contrast this implies to the life of the East. Here is a land where women are public, and where nobility in a man is best expressed by being handy about the house.

I tramped along the north side of St. Joseph's River, through beautiful country under delightful conditions. The corn-fields had turned red-gold, the grass was all in flower, and little brown fluffy bees considered it the best time of summer. What a sun there was, what a breeze! I found the "Bachelor's Retreat" on the St. Joseph's River, two boat-houses, a stairway through the forest banks, and a little wooden pier stretching out into the pleasant water—a good place for a swim!

Just before Mishewaka I met old Samuel Judie, seventy-six years of age, lying on a bank with a stick in his hand, tending the cows of his own farm and philosophising on life.

"It's a marvellous thing that the sun stands still and the earth goes round it," said he. "A marvellous thing that there are stars. They find out how to make automobiles, and they find out lots of things about the stars, but the human race won't ever know out the facts."

To most of the remarks I made Mr. Judie answered " Shah."

" England has fifty million people."

" Oh, shah ! "

" London is twenty miles broad and twenty miles long."

" Oh, shah ! "

" There are plenty of farms of only ten acres."

" Oh, shah ! "

He grumbled a great deal at the automobiles.

" Last Sunday," said he, " a man and his wife were knocked down just here. They had been saving and pinching for years, and had at last cleared the mortgage off their farm, and were reckoning to live decently. The automobile cut the woman's head right off, and the man is lying in the hospital. There ought to be a law against the automobiles rushing through from Elkhart to South Bend on Sundays."

" I suppose South Bend is a rich place ? "

" Shah ! "

" What do they make there ? "

" Boots, waggons, ploughs, the wooden parts of Singer's sewing-machines. . . . They are terribly hard up for hands. . . . You'd get a job easy. . . . There is a great lot of girls working in the factories, many foreign. They soon marry and go on to a farm. Factory folks make a pile of money ; get tired, and then buy a few acres of land and live on it. Farms about here are split up into small portions and sold to poor folk. Some want me to divide up my farm and sell part of it, but I won't do it."

Mr. Judie had had to work all his life, and to work hard a good deal of it, and he felt entitled to have his own mind on any subject, and to act accordingly.

A wealthy American took me along in his car through Mishewaka to South Bend, and showed me the great factory of wind-mill sails, Dodge's factory of " transmission power " of pulleys and connections and all things that join up engines and plant; then the famous Studebaker's factory of plough-handles, shafts, waggons, etc., the rubber-boot factory, Singer's frame factory, and several other establishments which indicated how busy these Indiana cities are.

I tramped out to New Carlisle, spending a night there under a deep dark maple tree, which after sunset looked like a great overlapping thatch—not a poke of light came through. As I lay beside the high road, and as the American holidays had just commenced, scores of cars came by, and as each one appeared on the road horizon it lit up my leafy ceiling with its great flashlights. How hot the night was. . . . I slept without covering. It was hot even at dawn.

It was next day on the road to Michigan City that I gave water to a thirsty calf, who actually ran to me and butted into me to persuade me to fill his bucket. It was on this road that having thrown a potful of water at some sheep they followed me down the dusty road, crying to me to do it again.

Michigan City was sweltering. I took refuge from the heat in the waiting-room of the large railway-station, and watched the crowds in the New York and Chicago trains, and the rush of the restaurant boys with hundreds of cones of ice-cream.

A pretty negress came and sat next me and began talking.

" Ah come over heer two manths ago to the carnaval, and have been playing *vaudy-ville*, but the home folks said ah mus' come back. Mai, how I cried when I heard. I did take on. . . ."

She was under police supervision, and a big Irish police-
8

man came and took her away when he saw her talking with me. She stood on the platform until the train came in, and then she was put in charge of a guard. She had, no doubt, been arrested under suspicious circumstances in the streets of Michigan, and had been brought before a kind magistrate, who had forborne to punish her on condition that she went back to her mother.

The road from Michigan undulated over a weedy wilderness and gnat-swarming marshes. I had a bad time as to the heat and the mosquitoes, and, despite use of strong disinfectants, I got badly stung, and was consequently feverish for some days. I was also very idle, very much inclined to sit on palings and consider how hot it was. On the Sunday, just to see whether the plaints of the farmers were justified, I made a census of all the vehicles that passed me. On the Monday I got to Hammond, and on Tuesday came in by car to Chicago. That day was the hottest of the year. Fifty-three people died from the heat in the city that day. I could have understood a few tramps dying even on the road.

XVI.

THE CHOIR DANCE OF THE RACES.

THE road into Chicago was one of increasing noise and smoke and desolation, of heat and gloom, and the rumour of a sordid defeat of life. I remember Calumet City by the factory stacks, the chimneys whose blackness seemed fainting out of sight in the haze of the heat. Dark smokes and white steams curled above many workshops; along the roadside black rivulets flowed from the factories. There were heaps of ashes and tin cans lying in odorous ponds. The leaves of the trees and the grasses of the fields were wilted and yellowed by the airs and fumes of Chicago. At Hammond a drunken, one-armed man followed me for about a mile, attracting a crowd of street Arabs by his foul language. East Chicago looked to me like parts of suburban London, and I was reminded in turns of Peckham, Hackney Marshes, Commercial Road, Whitechapel. There was, however, much that was unlike anything in London—the ominous squads of factory chimneys; clouds of heavy-rolling, ochreous fumes and smoke; palings with such advertisements as " Read no scab newspapers " or " You'll Holler "; wooden houses; dilapidated, ramshackle frame-buildings of grey wood; broken-down verandahs; black stairways; grey washing hanging on strings from stair-way to stairway; half-naked children; piles of old cans and rusty iron.

The vehicles increased on the highway, the lumber of

much traffic commenced, the red and yellow tramcars multiplied, railway lines crossed the road, and by the rush of trains one felt that all the traffic of Eastern and Central America was converging to one point. The open country disappeared. The air of the roadway became full of dust. The heat increased ten degrees, and to move a limb was to perspire. Foreigners jostled one another on the sidewalks, negroes and negresses sat in doorways. The odour of carcases came to the nostrils from Packing-town, and at last the great central roar of traffic—Chicago.

I can give no account of the great city here—it would be only to recount and add together the uglinesses and the promises of other cities. It was at once worse and better than I had expected. The hopelessness of the picture given by Upton Sinclair in *The Jungle* I felt to be exaggerated. I was told at Hull House that the novelist had got all his stories at the stockyards, but that the massed calamities that are so appalling in the story never occurred to one family in real life. The effect of accumulated horrible detail in *The Jungle* deprives you at the time of any love towards America ; it made me, a Briton, feel hatred towards America, and when first I read the book I felt that no Russian who read it carefully would entertain willingly the idea of going to America. If he had entertained the idea, having read *The Jungle* he would abandon it. It is an astonishing tract on the fate of a Russian peasant family leaving the land of so-called tyranny for a land of so-called freedom ; and its obvious moral is that Russia is a better country for the individual than America—that America takes the fine peasant stock of Europe and shatters it to bits.

It is true that Chicago makes a convenience of men, and that there man exists that commerce may thrive rather than that commerce exists that man may thrive. It is a place where the physical and psychical savings of Europeans are wasted like water, and where no one understands what the waste means. Spending is always joyful, and Chicago is a gay city. It is full of a light-hearted people, pushing, bantering, laughing, blindfolded over their spiritual eyes. In such places as Chicago the immigrant finds a market for things he could never sell at home—his body, his nerve, his vital energy ; a ready market, and he sells them and has money in his pocket and beer in plenty.   Listen to the loud-voiced, God-invoking crowd in the saloons ! They have the proceeds that come of selling the savings of Europe. They have come out of the quiet villages and forests where, from generation to generation and age to age, the peasantry live quiet lives, and grow richer and richer in spirit and nerve.   But these in the Chicago streets and saloons have found their mysterious destiny, to lavish in a life, and for seemingly worthless ends, what hundreds of quiet-living ancestors have saved.   The tree of a hundred years falls in a day and becomes timber, supporting a part of the fabric of civilisation for a while.

The strangest thing is the clamour of the Chicago crowd —it is dead-sure about everything in the world, ignorant, cocksure, mocking.   It does not know it is losing, does not know that it is blindfolded, because it is the victim of destiny.

Part of the spiritual blindness of the great city is the belief it holds that there is no other place of importance but itself.   And many outsiders take the city at its own estimate. But Chicago is not America, neither is New York or any other great city.   If going to America meant going only to the great cities, then few but the Jews would emigrate from Europe.

The ideals of America cannot be worked out merely in the great cities. The cities are places of death, of the destruction of national tissue, and of human combustion, necessary, no doubt, as such, certainly not places where one need worry about national health. The national health is on the farms of Pennsylvania and Indiana and Minnesota, Michigan, Iowa, the Dakotas, the Far West. The men range big out there ; the stand-by of the people will always be found in these places and not in the cities.

And New York and Chicago, though necessary, are abnormal. They are not so much America as unassimilated Europe. The population of a city should be the natural sacrifice of the population of the country. It is often deplored that the country people are forsaking the land and flocking to the towns ; but the proper people to replenish the failing stock of the cities is just those whom instinct and destiny prompt to leave the country. It is most bewildering to the student of America that her city-populations are replenished by the foreign immigrants, by people nursing, it is true, American sentiments, but not yet born into the American ideal, not made America's own. The natural place for the first generation of immigrants is on the land. If Chicago seems too large, too sudden a growth, disorderly, unanticipated, altogether out of hand, it is because of the hordes of foreigners who are there, who have not the impulse to co-operate, and who do not readily respond to the efforts of the idealist and politician. And they do not readily respond because they have not lived long enough in the true American atmosphere, have not served a quiet apprenticeship in the country, but have been dumped into an industrial wilderness served with the yellow press and " sped up."

America will have to guide the flow of the immigrants, and learn to irrigate with it and make fertile the middle and the far West. It is over-commercialisation and near-sightedness that clamours for more labour in the great cities. The size of a city is never too small. In the normal state of a nation the city functionises the country, and according to the strength of the people in the background the state of the great town will be busy or slack. It is good news that negotiations are being made with the trans-Atlantic shipping companies to ship immigrants to the Far Western coast *via* the Panama Canal, at rates not very much heavier than at present exist for shipment to Boston and Philadelphia and New York. A man and his wife planted on the land in the West are worth ten given to the greedy cities of the East.

In the matter of the colonisation of her own country America might learn a great deal from Russia, especially in the matter of railway transit. It is all to the advantage of a country that means of transit are cheap, and that there be a brisk circulation of the blood of the body-politic. As a newspaper realises that the cheaper its price the greater its success, the greater its circulation, so America might realise that the cheaper were its railway fares the more facility would there be for the mingling of the peoples, the assimilation of foreigners, and the development of the country.

In America it costs 39 dollars 60 cents to go as far as Denver, Colorado, which is about 2000 miles, and $76.20 to go to San Francisco. A comparison with the Russian rates will give an idea how much more cheaply it is possible to carry people :

Distance.	American Rates.	Russian Rates.		
		3rd Class.	4th Class.	Immigrants' Rate.
2000 miles	39.60 dollars	9 dollars	4.20 dollars	1 dollar
3230 „	76.20 „	12.50 „	6 „	1.60 dollars

Of course the cost of working is more in America than in Russia, and the trains are twice as fast ; but that is not enough to set off against the enormous differences in fares. A great profit is made out of the railway business, and the profit is at the expense of America as a whole. It is absurd to compare the prices of fares in America with the prices of fares in Great Britain. It is bad enough with us, but ours is a small territory ; it does not cost much to go from end to end. But America is a vast country. It costs almost a year's wages to pay the fare of a family across it. You think twice before determining to travel even a thousand miles. The consequence is that the circulation of people is sluggish in the extreme. The East begins to get congested, and the cities are packed with people who would gladly have gone straight to the West if facilities had been granted them.

In the development of democracy it is circulation that is important, the circulation of opinion, of sentiment, of ideals. The large circulation of interest and affection caused by the reduction of postage rates down to a penny in Britain and two cents in America has given an immense impetus to democratic development ; the larger circulation of ideas and opinions caused by the reduction of the price of newspapers to a cent has also been advantageous. But how much more important than the circulation of opinions, ideas, and sentiments is the circulation of the people themselves, controlled by the price of fares on railways ! How much more swiftly would the American democracy become homogeneous if it were possible to travel a thousand miles for five dollars. That would entail either nationalisation of railways or subsidisation by the Government. But it would be worth it to the American people.

Because of the heavy expense of railway travelling America is only dimly conscious of itself, geographically and ethnologically. Americans even boast of the distances between their towns and between different points of the country. Chicago, only one-third of the way across the continent, is called " The West." Indiana and Illinois and Minnesota are " out West." It is as if we referred to Berkshire or Warwickshire as the West of England.

In due course, it may be imagined, the United States Government will assume state-control of many of the railways, and ten dollars will pay your fare from New York right across. Immigrants will not be allowed to settle in great cities till they have spent ten years on the land. Such a provision would make it easier to admit all sorts and conditions of Europeans at Ellis Island ; and at the corresponding immigration stations at other ports a great deal of the White Slave trouble would be averted, and the shelter of immigrants would not absorb so much of the urban attention so urgently needed elsewhere.

.   .   .   .   .   .

Railways have as much power to make the new American as the newspaper has. Perhaps they have more power ; for the railways can afford great opportunities for social mingling. The railway can take any immigrant to a place where he will be not merely a hireling, but a living organism grafted into the vast body of America. At present the high fares deter the immigrant, and he is cooped up in districts which he would like to leave, but cannot ; in districts where he must remain foreign and not American.

For there is an impulse to move and to mingle. If railway facilities were granted there would be a great deal more social and commercial intercourse over the surface of America. Each new immigrant who comes into the United States is particularly wanted somewhere ; his landing is not an accident. Some village or country-side has called him, and will still call him, though he be frustrated at first, doing the wrong sort of work among the wrong group of people.

The great heterogeneous mass of peoples wants to become one nation. There is a power which works through the peoples for that end. The people are ready to mingle; they are already mingling; they are going to and fro and in two and threes, and every step and every transaction is something essential in the making of the coming homogeneous nation.

It is a choir dance, a dance of molecules or atoms, if you will, but a dance of human atoms, and one that yields a mystic music that can be heard by the poet's ear. Leading the peoples in the involutions and evolutions of the choir dance is a masked figure, not itself one of the people. What is that figure? Not trade, I think, though it helps; not common interest, though it is perhaps a rule of the dance; not even the American idea. The masked figure that leads is a fate; it is an instinct of Destiny.

The dance is being played out on a vast stage with much scenery—the three-thousand-mile stretch of America, East to West: the Industrial East, with its hills; the corn plains and forests of the middle West; the wild West; the luxuriant and wonderful South.

There are waiting throngs cooped up in cities and at temporary standing-places.

The welter of negroes and Spaniards and half-castes in the South, in the black pale; the Swedes and Norwegians and Finns in the middle West; the million Jews in New York; the millions of them elsewhere, saying, as Mary Antin, that America and not Judea is the Promised Land, the place where the tribes will be gathered together again and form a nation; the great Anglo-Saxon stock of America, who would feel themselves to be the leaven, the ruling principle in the choir dance; the Dutch-Americans of Pennsylvania; the Irish, of whom there tend to be more in America than in Ireland; the Slovaks and Ruthenians on the Pennsylvanian collieries; the Italian gangs on the road and the Italian quarters of a thousand towns; the Poles, of whom in New York alone there are more than in any city in Poland; the enormous number of Germans living on the land; the hundred thousand Russian working men in Pennsylvania alone; the Molokan Russians in California, and the Russian gold-washers; the Red Indians on the Reservations; the composite gangs of all nations in the world going up and down the country doing jobs.

The Jews bring music, mathematical instinct, a sense of justice, industry, commercial organisation and commercial tyranny, national wealth, material prosperity, restlessness.

The English bring ignorance, pluck, and honour; the Scottish bring their brains and their morals; the Irish bring generosity, cleverness, laziness, hatred of Jews and of meanness.

The Germans bring the idea of growth and development, evolution, and with it their own music. They also bring an instinct for efficiency and shining armour.

The negro brings sensual music and dancing, a taste for barbaric splendour, the gentleness of little children, and the wildness of the beasts of the forest at night; and he brings imitativeness, subserviency, a taste for slavery.

The Red Indians bring the remembrance of the Virgin Continent—litheness of limb, subtler ear and nose and eyes for the things of the earth.

The Italians bring their emotionalism and excitability, their songs, their passion, their fighting spirit.

The Little Russians, Slovaks, Poles, Great Russians

bring patience to endure suffering, but withal a spirit of anarchism which prompts them to do astonishing things without apparent cause, mystical piety, charity, much sin, much intemperance, much love and human tenderness. They bring also the Tartar commercial spirit, and a zest for haggling over prices and for making deals.

The French bring economy, vivacity, journalistic genius.

But what do they not bring, all these peoples ? There are marvellous gifts closed in all of them, mysterious potentialities that it were folly to attempt to name.

Each race has its special function, its organic suitability and psychic value. There are male races like the Jews ; female races like the Germans. There are races that bring spirit, races that bring body.

German goes down the middle with English ; Swedish with Irish ; Russian with Pole ; Jew with each and all. It is not always with the negro that the negro dances, not always with the Italian that the Italian is partnered, nor Hungarian with Hungarian, nor Lithuanian with Lithuanian. Secretively, unexpectedly, on unanticipated impulses, strangers obey the magic wand and rhythmical gestures of the Great Conductor of the dance, and become one with another in the evolution of America. The dance has been open some time, but it is only now becoming general. The waiting throngs on all sides are just beginning to break up and go mingling up and down and in and out, carrying messages, making sacrifices, performing rites. The victims are blindfolded ; the conquerors have the light of destiny on their brows.

A spectacle for the gods ! In the Old World the heavenly powers have looked down more or less on the antagonism of the races, war and enmity and all that results from great battles, the rout of armies, the sacking of cities, the sinking of ships—

Looking over wasted lands.
Blight and famine, plague and earthquake, roaring deeps and fiery sands,
Clanging fights, and flaming towns, and sinking ships, and praying hands.

But in the New World the peoples are joined in co-operation and friendship, working out in peace and trade the synthesis of a new race. The gods look down on factory-chimneys belching smoke, on kingdoms covered with red-gold corn uncoveted by men of arms, on hurrying trains and the dancing peoples going hither and thither, with smiles and little enchantments and allurements. They look upon the Protestant pulpits where the Puritans preach, on the Roman Catholic Church and the confessionals, on the Orthodox Church, on the Baptists, on the Mormons ; and on the way the varying peoples flock around temples, and in and out of church doors, carrying messages, receiving messages. They look upon many developments that we have so aptly called movements—the mysterious " woman's movement," the Romanising movement, the Socialistic movement. They look upon a million schools where the children, the second generation of the dancers, are polished and tested and clothed before they in their turn join the throng at the side and go down the middle with their partners.

It is like a kaleidoscope, and at each successive revolution the peoples change their aspects and their pattern ; but there is no reverting to the original pattern, as in the kaleidoscope. The constituents of the pattern are divining what the next pattern will be, and it is always a new pattern, something nearer to the great coming unity, the new American nation. In no one particular bosom is the destiny of America ; one man by himself means nothing there. It is a whole people that is living or will live. Once the foreigner parts from the waiting throngs at the side and enters the mystic dance, his own little consciousness and purpose become but a part of the much greater consciousness and purpose of the whole. It is not the development of one sort of person, but the combination of a million sorts to make one. It is not the development of a race, as is our own British progress in Great Britain, but something which seems rather novel in the history of mankind, the making of a new democracy. It is not a Gladstone or a Bismarck or an Alexander the Liberator, who is leading this development that I have called a Choir Dance, not a Lincoln or a Roosevelt or a Wilson. Men have only their parts to play in the making of a democracy; if they could make it all by themselves, or originate the making, or achieve the making, it would not be a democracy that they were making. As I said, it is a masked figure that leads the mystic movement—a fate. In one sense there are many fates also among the dancers and mingled with them,—a mysterious and wonderful ballet, perfect in idea and in fulfilment.

And as it is with men so it is with the rites they perform. There are myriads of rites in the movement of the dance, but not one of them is charged with absolute significance. Thus in the mazes of evolution there stands impregnable, as it would seem, the historic open Bible of America. Around it, marking time, is a massed host of Americans, now reinforced by newcomers, now diminished by secessions, swayed to this way and to that by streams of Catholics, streams of Hebrews, streams of pleasure-lovers, but as yet holding its own, and claiming in sonorous choruses that the Bible shall be the leaven of the New America.

At another point of vantage on the stage you may see the Jews proclaiming by vote that America is no longer a Christian country, and calling the intellectuals and pleasurewanters to support, if not Judaism, at least rationalism and " intelligent " materialism.

At another point you see the menace of the half-civilised negro, the spectacle of the rapid multiplication of a people over whom there is no control, and in whose nature lies, apparently, an enormous physical power to degrade the type of the whites.

There is the phenomenon of the wholesale slaughter and sacrifice of blindfolded foreigners exploited in industrial cities ; forests of men used up as the forests of wood are worn away into daily newspapers and rubbish.

You see the booths where dancers make voluntary abdication of European nationality and take the oaths of American citizenship.

You see the prizes for which, in the dance, whole crowds seem to be straining and yearning and even struggling, the prize of wealth, of even a little wealth, of a name printed in a newspaper, of a name printed in all newspapers, the prize of fame, of political position, of premiership. You see the wild political campaigns.

You see the places where the ambitious laze by the way, the baseball races where men are shouting themselves and others mad for an empty game, the halls of rag-time and trotting. You see in thousands of instances actions which seem to disgrace the name of America and to augur ill for her future,—women sold into evil, negroes burned at the stake, heinous crimes committed against children. But the destiny of the great choric dance cannot be thwarted by any of these things. Death is useful to life, darkness to brightness, sin to virtue—useful in a way which it is not necessary for the individual to penetrate. Each man fulfils his destiny, guides others according to his light, acts according to his inclination, temptation, and conscience. The whole nation takes care of itself.

• • • • • •

Wherever I went in the States I was asked by journalists to say what I thought the resultant type of American was going to be. America seemed feverishly anxious to get an answer to that question. No one can answer it, but it is exciting to speculate.

" Are you aware that in a few years we shall come to such a pass that it will be a stand-up fight, Americans *versus* Jews ? " said one man to me. " The influence of the other races goes for nothing beside the influence of the Jews. The Jews are buying up all the real estate, they make any sacrifice for education, they get the better of Christians nine times out of ten. A Jewish pedlar comes past this door one day, and I think, ' Poor wretch ! ' Next year he comes past in a buggy ; next year I find he owns a big general store in the town ; next year he owns a department store and employs a thousand hands. He is too much for us."

What is to be the emerging American ? At New York I was inclined to answer, " A sort of English-speaking Russian Jew who believes in dollars and sensual pleasures before all else, who, however, reads advanced literature, and whilst he is poor is an anarchist, and when he is rich is more tyrannous than the Tsar—more tyrannous, but never illegally so." But when I escaped into the country I found that New York was not America, but only a great hostelry on the threshold of that country. I learned the great control power of the Anglo-Saxon and Dutch Americans, the subtle influence of the Russian people, who after all not only dominate the Jews in Russia, but give them many traits of the Russian national character, making out of a materialist something which is almost a sentimentalist. There are many Jews in Russia who have become de-judaised by the Russians, and indeed the Christian Jew has become part of the very fabric of that bureaucracy which the poor persecuted mob of Hebrews hate and fear. The Russians are a strong influence in the development of the American. And the Germans and Norwegians and Swedes and Danes, who swiftly change to a species of American hardly distinguishable from the old Anglo-Saxon and Dutch type ? They cannot go for nothing ; they are not simply raw material, but are moulders and fashioners as well. The coming American will be a very recognisable relation of the Teutonic peoples. But he will, nevertheless, be clearly and decidedly different from any one race on the Continent.

Even to-day an American is distinctly recognisable as such on the pavements of London, Berlin, or Paris. You know him by his face ; he does not need to speak to reveal his nationality. You can even tell a man who has spent five years in the country ; something new has been moulded into his face and has crept into his eyes. I have even noticed it in the face of Russian peasants returning from America after two years away from Russia, travelling in a Russian train to their little village home.

" You are American ? " I asked of them.

" Yes, boss, you are rait," they replied, and smiled knowingly.

They then began to enlarge on what a wonderful place America was — just like American tourists in Switzerland.

But the American of to-day is not the American of to-morrow. The Tsar's subjects coming into America at the rate of a quarter of a million a year ensure that, the flocking of almost whole nations from South-Eastern Europe ensure it. As I said, none can tell what the new American nation will be. We can only watch the wonderful patterns and colours that form in the great ballet and choir dance, the mingling in the labyrinths of destiny, the disappearances and the emergencies, the involution and the evolution. It is something enacted within the mystery of the human race itself.

XVII.

FAREWELL, AMERICA!

I OBSERVED many interesting things in Chicago, the following circular for instance :

> Balsok aut John J. Casey.
> Hlasujte na John J. Casey.
> Glosujgie na John J. Casey.
> Votate per John J. Casey.
> Vote for John J. Casey,
> Labour candidate for Congress.

Ten years hence that farrago will have changed to simply " Vote for Casey."

My neighbours in the hotel spelt their name in two ways, one way for Polish friends and the other for American understanding :

> Nawrozke.
> Navrozky.

It is the latter name that will endure ; or perhaps that also will be shed for some cognomen that sounds more familiar and reliable,—to Harris or Jones or Brown.

I had a talk in a slum with a family of Roumanian Jews who had come to Chicago twenty years ago. Chicago was a good place, they intended never to leave it, the family had come there for ever.

I met an Alsatian who told me how he had fled from home when he was twelve years old. He crossed the

Swiss frontier, and got into Basle at midnight, and had travelled to America *via* Paris and Havre, and had never gone back. He did not want to serve in the German Army. His father had been a great French soldier in the Franco-German war.

" If you went back now would the German authorities bring you to trial ? " I asked.

" No. I have the Emperor's pardon in black and white."

" Do many of those who run away get pardon ? "

" Only when there is good cause. I used to send money home regularly to keep my sister. The mayor of the town heard of my generosity, reported it to Berlin, and a pardon was written out for me."

" They thought it a pity to keep a good citizen out of his own country, even though he had cheated the army. A wise action, eh ? " said I.

" The Germans are 'cute," he replied.

I met a Russian revolutionary who complained that his compatriots in the towns spent all their spare time getting drunk, fighting, and praying. The Russian who made his pile went and opened a beer-shop. He thought the priests of the Orthodox Church kept the immigrants down ; they got more money from drunkards than from the virtuous, and therefore they made no efforts to encourage sobriety. He would like to see the Orthodox Greek and Russian Churches demolished, and the priests and deacons packed back to Europe. America was a new country, and needed a new church.

At Chicago also I received a letter from Andray Dubovoy, a young Russian farmer, whose acquaintance I made by chance in the Russian quarter of New York. He was rich enough to come travelling from North Dakota to New York to see the sights of America, a wonderfully keen and happy Russian, full of ideas about the future and stories of the settlement where he lived. He gave me a most interesting account of the Russian pioneers in North Dakota. In the towns where he lived every one spoke Russian, and few spoke English. If you went into a shop and asked for something in English the shopkeeper would shrug her shoulders and send for a little child to interpret. The children went to school and knew English, but the old folks could not master it, and had long given up attempts to learn the language. The town was called Kief, and was named after the province of Russia from which they originally came.

He told me the history of two villages in Kiefsky Government in Russia. They had heard of America, but thought it was a place in a fairy-tale—not a real place at all. They were even incredulous when the Jews began to depart for America in numbers. But they were destined to understand.

The villagers were people who asked themselves serious questions and searched their hearts. They ceased going to monasteries and making pilgrimages and kissing relics, and instead gathered together and read the Gospel.

Many were arrested for going to illegal meetings. Those who were sent to prison or to Siberia went gladly, as on the Lord's business, to be missionaries to those who sat in darkness.

But there was so much persecution that a great number of the villagers thought of following the example of the Jews and emigrating to America. It was in 1894 that they resolved to go ; but at that time a large party of Stundists, who had gone out to Virginia the year before, came back with tidings of bad life and poor wages, and damped the enthusiasm. Ten families, however, were tempted by what the Stundists said, and they took tickets to go to the very district of Virginia that the Stundists had abandoned.

On their way out they fell in with a party of German colonists going back, after a holiday, to North Dakota. Such tales they told that five of the families changed their minds and determined to throw in their lot with the Germans.

The five families received land free, homesteads, they were given credit to purchase horses and cattle and carts and agricultural implements, and they liked the new country and wrote glowingly to the others in Virginia and in the two villages of Kiefsky Government. As a result, twenty-five new families came at once, and in a few years there were 200 families installed.

Each man brought 20 to 30 dollars but no more, and each became indebted to companies for 1000 to 1500 dollars, a debt which they hoped to pay, but which hung on their necks like the instalments their ancestors had to pay to the Land Banks of Russia for the land they had been granted.

However, they ploughed and sowed and hoped for harvests, built log cabins and even American houses. They had hard times, and were on the verge of starvation— famine and death staring at them from the barren fields. They were forced to make an appeal through the newspapers of Eastern America, and as a result truck-loads of provisions were sent to them, and " clothes to last five years."

Succeeding years made up for their sufferings. There was a plentiful flax harvest ; and though in 1909 hail destroyed the wheat and in 1910 and 1911 there was drought, the Russians bore up. And 1912 was a most fruitful year, some farmers garnering as many as 25,000 bushels of wheat.

Each year they were able to add to their stock, to build a little more, and to do various things. As a result of good harvests Andray Dubovoy himself was able to go a-travelling, and to meet me and tell me his story. He had himself come to America when a little child, and did not know of his native land except by repute. He had not, however, had the advantage of education in an American school as a child, and so was as yet more Russian than American; but he was unlike the Russian type, he was clean of limb, clear of eye and of skin, calm—almost a Quaker in faith and morals. No one drank spirits or smoked tobacco in Kief, North Dakota, he told me with pride. The Russians there were living in a new way.

"Are the people as religious now as they were in Russia?" I asked.

"Not quite," said he, "they feel they don't need religion so much in America. At first the struggle for life was so hard, we had little thought for religion. It was only as we gained a footing on the land that we began to think of our religion seriously, and we built a chapel. We have a chapel of our own now."

"I suppose when you were no longer persecuted you did not need to affirm your way of religion so emphatically," I hazarded.

Andray did not know.

"Have you any bosses in Kief?" I asked.

Andray smiled.

"Our sheriff is a cabman."

"You feel no tyranny at all now?"

He was glad to say they never had need of a policeman; there were no robberies, every one lived in mutual love and kindness. Only, of course, they were heavily in debt to the companies, and felt they were never solvent.

"Perhaps, when you have improved your land and made it really valuable you will be sold up by the companies and you will lose your property," said I.

He did not think that possible.

"And what is the cost of living with you?"

"Cheap," said my friend; "beef is 2½ cents a pound, eggs 10 cents the dozen, butter 12 cents the pound, potatoes 35 cents the bushel; but the things we import, such as boots, clothes, fruits, are very dear, much too dear for our pockets."

"Food is cheaper than in the country in Russia, then?"

"Meat and butter and milk are cheaper, but other things are more than twice as dear. Still we do not complain. It is a good life out there; our children are growing up stalwart, happy, earnest. God's own blessing is upon our enterprise."

"Are you ever going back to Russia with its persecutions, its sins, its crimes, its pilgrimages, the secret police, the hermits who live in forest huts, its moujiks and babas, who think that America is a place in a fairy-tale, at the other side of endless forests?"

The farmer smiled in a peculiar way. He would like to go to see it.

Was he quite sure he was going to be an American and not a Russian?

"We have Russian classes in the summer," said he. "We must never forget Russia, evil as she is."

. . . . . .

It must not be forgotten that this little settlement of which I write here is only one of many in North Dakota. There are already thirty thousand Russians living in that state, and there are many people of other nationalities living in the same way—Swedes, Germans, Danes. The story of the young colonies is marvellously touching; when you read one of the excellent novels of to-day, such as Miss Cather's *O Pioneers*, which tells of the growth of a Swedish colony in the middle-west, you are obliged to admit that it is no wonder the Americans find their own such an exclusively interesting country.

. . . . . .

I returned to New York by train, and on the way saw the Niagara Falls, one morning at dawn ; the procession of white-headed rapids, the vapour and mist rising in volumes veiling the sun, darkening it. A sight of holiness and wonder that left me breathless. I was glad to be alone, and just close the picture into the heart, in silence !

Late one Saturday night I arrived in New York and stepped out of the Great Central Station, pack on back, and searched for a hotel. The grand " Knickerbocker," with sky-sign the length of the Great Bear, was not for me. I wandered into a queer-looking little palace, all mirrors, deep carpets, white paint, and niggers. My room faced the street, and opposite me was a pleasure-resort, a cabaret, a dance-hall, a pool-house, with three stories of billiard-rooms, through whose open windows I saw many white-sleeved billiard-players leaning over green tables.

The weather was so hot that all the windows in the city were wide open. I heard the throbbing of music and dancing, even in my dreams.

Some days later I booked my passage back to England. But I was in America till the last moment. The American who was so kind to me, and who was in herself a little America, " fed to me " daily the facts of American life, and the hope of all those who were working with her. We visited Patterson, where half a dozen " Jim Larkins " had been fighting for fighting's sake, and leading the well-paid silk-workers to strike for the sun and moon, and accept no compromise. We visited the President of the City College and saw the wonderful modern equipment of that institution. We called on J. Cotton Dana, the librarian of Newark. I was enabled to visit a maternity hospital, heavily endowed by Pierpont Morgan, and to see all the provision made for the happy birth of the emerging Americans. One vision remains in my memory of a dozen babies on a tray, each baby having its mother's name written on a piece of paper pinned to its swaddling-bands.

We visited five or six settlements, and invitations were given me to visit several thousand establishments in the United States, and miss nothing. I would have liked to go farther afield and have a thousand more conversations, but perhaps, since brevity is the soul of wit, I have done enough. As it is, I have only made a small selection of instances and adventures and thoughts from the immense amount of material which I carried back to England and to Russia. I think America has been brought to the touch-stone of my own intelligence, experience, and personality.

. . . . . .

My friend took me to the charming play, *Peg-o'-my-Heart*.

" Isn't it delicious ? "

" The thrilling thing is that the fifth act is not played out here, but on the *Campania*, and I have to play that part myself," said I.

We got out of the theatre at eleven. I saw her home. As midnight was striking I claimed my luggage at the cloak-room at Christopher Street Ferry. At 12.15 I entered the Cunard Dock and saw the great, washed-over, shadowy, twenty-year-old Atlantic Liner. Crowds of drunkards were gesticulating and waving flags—Stars and Stripes and Union Jacks—singing songs, embracing one another. Heavily laden dock-porters, carrying sacks, moved in procession along the gangways. Portly Chief Steward Macrady, with mutton-chop whiskers, weather-beaten face, and wordless lips, sat in his little kiosk and motioned to me to pass on when I showed my ticket. I got aboard.

I returned with the home-going tide of immigrants; with flocks of Irish who were going boisterously back to

the Green Isle to spend small fortunes ; with Russians returning to Russia because their time was up and they were
due to serve in the army ; with British rolling-stones,
grumbling at all countries ; with people going home because
they were ill ; with men and women returning to see aged
fathers or mothers ; with a whole American family going
from Butte, Montana, to settle in Newcastle, England.

It was a placid six-day voyage ; six days of merriment,
relaxation, and happiness. The atmosphere was entirely
a holiday one—not one of hope and anxiety and faith, as
that of going out had been. Every one had money, almost
every one was a person who had succeeded, who had tall
tales to tell when he got home to his native village in his
native hollow.

Thousands of opinions were expressed about America.
I heard few of disillusion. Most people who go to America
are disillusioned sooner or later, but they re-catch their
dreams and illusions, and gild their memories when they
set sail upon the Atlantic once more. They have become
Americans, and have a stake in America, and are ready to
back the New World against anything in the Old.

" Do you like the Yankees ? "

" They're all right—on the level," answers an Irish boy.

" Do you like America ?   Would you like to live there
and settle down there ? " asks a friend of me, the wanderer.

A smile answers that question.

We stood, my friend and I, looking over the placid
ocean as the moon just pierced the clouds and glimmered
on the waters.

Evening splendours were upon the surface of the sea,
the delicate light of the moon just showing the waves, most
beautiful and alluring.

" It is like first acquaintance with one's beloved," said
I ; " like the first smile that life gives you, bidding you

follow her and woo her. Later on, in the rich splendour, when the golden road is clear and certain and ours, we do not care for the quest. We look back to those first enchanting glances, those promising reconnaissances. The promise of love is more precious than love itself, for it promises more than itself ; it promises the unearthly ; it touches a note of a song that we heard once, and have been all our lives aching to remember and sing again."

America is too happy and certain and prosperous a place for some. It is a place where the soul falls into a happy sleep. The more America improves, the more will it prove a place of success, of material well-being, of physical health, and sound, eugenically established men and women. But to me, personally, success is a reproach ; and failure, danger, calamity, incertitude is a glory. For this world is not a satisfying home, and there are those who confess themselves strangers and pilgrims upon the earth.

. . . . .

Back to Russia ! From the most forward country to the most backward country in the world ; from the place where " time is money " to where the trains run at eighteen miles an hour ; from the land of Edison to the land of Tolstoy ; from the religion of philanthropy to the religion of suffering—home once more.

INDEX.

THE END.

PRINTED IN GREAT BRITAIN AT
THE PRESS OF THE PUBLISHERS.

Established 1798

T. NELSON
& SONS, Ltd.
PRINTERS AND
PUBLISHERS